PREACHING
RESURRECTION

Preaching Classic Texts

Preaching Apocalyptic Texts
Larry Paul Jones and Jerry L. Sumney

Preaching Job
John C. Holbert

Preaching Luke-Acts
Ronald J. Allen

Preaching Resurrection
O. Wesley Allen, Jr.

PREACHING
RESURRECTION

O. WESLEY
ALLEN, JR.

St. Louis, Missouri

Scripture quotations, unless otherwise noted, are author's translations.

Scripture quotations marked NRSV are from the *New Revised Standard Version Bible*, copyright 1989, Division of Christian Education of the National Council of the Churches of Christ in the United States of America. Used by permission. All rights reserved.

Cover Art: Erich Lessing/Art Resource, N.Y. "The Angel Opening Christ's Sepulchre," Museum of Fine Arts, Budapest, Hungary
Cover Design: Michael Foley
Interior design: Wynn Younker
Art Director: Michael A. Domínguez

This book is printed on acid-free, recycled paper.

Visit Chalice Press on the World Wide Web at
www.chalicepress.com

10 9 8 7 6 5 4 3 2 1   00 01 02 03

Library of Congress Cataloging–in–Publication Data

Allen, O. Wesley, 1965-
   Preaching resurrection / O. Wesley Allen, Jr. /
    p.   cm. – (Preaching classic texts)
   Includes bibliographical references.
   ISBN 0-8272-2961-5
   1. Preaching. 2. Jesus Christ–Resurrection. 3. Jesus Christ–Passion. I. Title. II. Series.
BV4211.5 A44 2000
232' .5–dc21   00-010031
                                                                      CIP

Printed in the United States of America

Russell J. Compton, Professor Emeritus of Philosophy and Religion
at DePauw University,
has offered critique of the shallowness
of most Easter sermons he has heard throughout his 92 years of life.
His most precise words were, "Easter is the dullest Sunday of the
year."
This critique has inspired me
to strive to preach the resurrection
with more depth and relevance for modern existence
and indeed to write this book.
And I know of no one who has exhibited more depth and relevance
in applying the good news of Jesus Christ
to the struggles and joys of human existence than has Russell.

In appreciation for his role as mentor, colleague, friend, and saint,
I dedicate this book to him.

CONTENTS

PREFACE

Preaching in today's postmodern, indeed post-Christian, culture is no easy task. It is hard enough to preach on the run-of-the-mill Sunday, when I am proclaiming the good news to the faithful with whom I worship week in and week out. But it is even harder on Easter Sunday, when the pews are filled with those who come only once or twice a year. They come on this day because they know that the proclamation that Jesus Christ is risen from the dead is central to the Christian faith, a faith they claim as their own even if they don't choose to regularly practice it in the context of community. They hope that what I have to say, along with the liturgy and music, will make that proclamation real for them.

I set upon the task of writing this book to help me struggle with the call to be a better preacher on Easter Sunday and every time the Body of Christ gathers to worship in celebration of the resurrection of Jesus Christ. I set upon the task because I strongly desire to make the stories of the resurrection of Jesus Christ real for today's Christians, and by *real* I mean evident in their lives and in their world *today.* Choosing to face this struggle by writing a book, of course, implies that I think other preachers share my struggle and that I hope my reflections on the resurrection narratives may be of some help in fulfilling their call.

The goal of the book is to help us preachers take a new look at the resurrection narratives. Its aim is to hint at the myriad connections between the stories of the resurrection of Jesus Christ and our stories of existence in the early twenty-first century. In short, its purpose is to enhance and even transform what is heard from pulpits on Easter Sunday.

The book strives to meet this goal with three approaches. This first approach is general in nature. In a brief introduction, I attempt to deal with some broad issues related to preaching the resurrection narratives in general in today's world. The second approach is exegetical in nature. I offer an interpretation of each gospel's version of the resurrection. By placing each version of the resurrection of Jesus Christ in its narrative and theological context, it is my hope that the unique characteristics of each story will come to light. If this is achieved, then we should be able to identify ways that we preach the resurrection differently when we are looking at Matthew's gospel than when we are speaking about John's. The third approach is homiletical in nature. Following each exegesis chapter is an example sermon on the individual gospel resurrection narratives (two sermons are offered for John). These sermons in no way represent an attempt to encompass all that is highlighted in the exegetical discussions, but instead are examples of focusing on a particular aspect of a particular version of the Easter story for a particular liturgical occasion.

Because my goal is to serve as a resource for the pulpit and not to enter into debate concerning the scholarly analysis of the gospel narratives, I have chosen not to include detailed footnotes in the midst of the exegetical chapters. Instead, a bibliography of resources that may be useful to preachers who wish to pursue this subject in greater depth is included at the end of the work.

Before moving on, it would be inappropriate not to pause briefly and acknowledge those who have helped bring this book into being. Jon L. Berquist, my editor at Chalice Press, has been an essential conversation partner as I struggled with various issues of content and has exhibited great patience with me as deadlines passed. Deborah Chew, my secretary, has handled numerous administrative details related to the book, not the least of which was protecting my backup files with her life. And Bonnie Cook and Maggie Cook-Allen, my wife and my daughter, have inspired me as I reflect on the meaning of life expressed in the stories of the resurrection.

Wes Allen
Easter 2000

CHAPTER 1

Introduction

This book offers a literary-theological interpretation of the Easter narratives that is intended to be a resource for preaching the resurrection narratives from early twenty-first century pulpits. With all the renewed interest in the quest for the historical Jesus, however, it is also important to claim from the outset what the book is not. It is not an attempt to address the question of the historicity of the resurrection of Jesus. The book's focus on the task of preaching the resurrection narratives does not ask readers to decide whether they believe in the historicity of the resurrection or not.

Nevertheless, if the discussions and sermons that follow are to serve as useful conversation partners for preachers, readers must be willing to consider that the meaning of the resurrection of Jesus Christ for today's Christians (or for Christians of any other era) is not primarily grounded in the historical question. They must be willing to consider that the act of claiming the stories of the resurrection of Jesus Christ as significant for revealing the nature of existence today need not be rooted in historical assumptions about an ancient resuscitation of the corpse of Jesus of Nazareth. They must be willing to consider that, while history and theology are deeply interconnected, historical investigation is not the primary category for theological inquiry.

Stated from a different angle, this book is written for those who think that we who are engaged in theological inquiry and spiritual journeys acquire a sense of direction from the past while charting our course based on our present experience of Ultimate Meaning in the world and future hope for the world rooted in faith in God. It is written for those who wish to proclaim the core of the good news of Jesus Christ as being the claim that Christ *is* risen, not the claim that Jesus *was* risen. It is for those who ask what the Easter narratives offer today's Christian communities and for individuals seeking to grow in their understanding of Ultimate Reality, self, and world. It is for those who want to know what the stories offer us when we wish to have a significant impact on today's world in the name of the risen Christ.

To meet the needs of such readers, the book will focus on the New Testament texts that proclaim and interpret the story of the resurrection of Jesus Christ. While the resurrection is a theme that plays a role in almost every writing of the New Testament, stories of the resurrection appear only five times: at the end of each of the four gospels and in 1 Corinthians 15: 3–8. But whereas the four gospels recount the story of the resurrection as a key element of their proclamation of the Christ Event (i.e., they tell their stories of the resurrection for their own sake), Paul uses the Easter tradition he has inherited and passed on for two different purposes. Let us look at 1 Corinthians 15:3–12:

> For I handed on to you as of first importance what I in turn had received: that Christ died for our sins in accordance with the scriptures, and that he was buried, and that he was raised on the third day in accordance with the scriptures, and that he appeared to Cephas, then to the twelve. Then he appeared to more than five hundred brothers and sisters at one time, most of whom are still alive, though some have died. Then he appeared to James, then to all the apostles. Last of all, as to one untimely born, he appeared also to me. For I am the least of the apostles, unfit to be called an apostle, because I persecuted the church of God. But by the

grace of God I am what I am, and his grace toward me has not been in vain. On the contrary, I worked harder than any of them–though it was not I, but the grace of God that is with me. Whether then it was I or they, so we proclaim and so you have come to believe.

Now if Christ is proclaimed as raised from the dead, how can some of you say there is no resurrection of the dead? (NRSV)

The first purpose for which Paul recites the tradition of Christ's resurrection is found in verses 8–11 and is secondary to the focus of the rest of the chapter. The fact that Christ appeared to him, albeit "last of all," is offered as a validation of his role as an apostle and, therefore, of his authority to address the tensions dealing with doctrine and practice in the Corinthian church. This validation prepares Paul's original readers to accept what he argues in the rest of the chapter.

The second reason that Paul reminds his readers of the Easter tradition that he proclaimed to them is to address one of those doctrinal issues that is in dispute among the Corinthian house churches, that of the resurrection of the body. This issue rises to the surface in verse 12 and remains the focus throughout the rest of the chapter. Paul is arguing against those in Corinth who have a realized eschatology and claim that they have already experienced the resurrection of the dead. His argument for the resurrection of the body and his interpretation of the doctrine is extremely complex and need not concern us. For our purposes, it is simply important to note that in 1 Corinthians 15 Paul does not *proclaim* the resurrection power of Jesus Christ; he *refers* to the proclamation of the resurrection of Jesus Christ as a means of (or a basis for) diving into a different (but obviously related) pool.

First Corinthians 15 is an important text for understanding Pauline theology and indeed for catching a glimpse of a first-century Christian debate concerning the nature of eschatology and eternal life. Moreover, 1 Corinthians 15:3–8 is an essential text to examine if one is investigating historical issues related to the resurrection or if one is examining the historical development of the resurrection traditions. But because the purpose of this book is to serve as a resource for those preaching the stories of the resurrection of Jesus Christ, we will focus our attention on the four versions of the Easter story that are found in the gospels.

The Story of the Resurrection in Today's Pulpit

A preacher stepped into the pulpit one week and asked his congregation to indicate whether they already knew what he was going to say to them. They, of course, said that they did not. To this the preacher replied, "Then of what use to you or to me is an unknown subject?" Then he descended from the pulpit and left the mosque.

The following Friday the preacher asked a larger congregation the same question. This time, however, the congregation had prepared beforehand and responded that they did know what he was going to say. Then the preacher replied, "That being the case, there is no need either of wasting your time or of wasting mine," and he descended from the pulpit and left the mosque.

A week later the preacher again mounted the pulpit and asked whether the even larger congregation already knew what he was going to say. Having once again prepared beforehand, half the congregation claimed that they did know what he planned to say, and half claimed that they did not. At this point, the preacher said, "It is well said; and now if the half that knows what I am going to say would explain to the other half what it is, I would be deeply grateful, for it will be unnecessary for me to say anything." Then the preacher descended from the pulpit and left the mosque.[1]

Both preachers and congregations on Easter Sunday should be able to relate to this story. Too many preachers enter the pulpit on Easter morning and try to place their congregations back in an ancient cemetery and surprise them with the discovery of an empty tomb. The problem is that there is rarely a single person over the age of twelve in worship on Easter Sunday who does not already know what the preacher is going to say, who does not already know the basic story of the resurrection. That is, after all, why so many people attend worship on Easter, even if they do not come the rest of the year. They probably don't know the differences between the four gospels' accounts of the resurrection, but they know that when the women arrive, the tomb is empty. They know the basic story and that the Easter story is central to the Christian faith. They know that it is supposed to be important to their own faith. What many do not know is in what way the claim that Christ is risen should actually inform their existence and their worldview. Therefore, they come to worship on Easter morning both because they already know the story and because they want to hear something new from this story that they already know. If preachers surprise their congregations by offering them a meaningful vision of the reality of and hope for the resurrection of Jesus Christ in their own lives and in the contemporary world in which they live, sanctuaries will begin to fill on the Sunday after Easter as well as on Easter Sunday.

The goal of a sermon, any sermon, is to offer a vision of a particular aspect of Christian reality and Christian existence, a vision that is drawn from scripture (and ecclesial tradition) and is informed by critical forms of contemporary knowledge and experience, a vision that is concrete enough to be assimilated into the very being of the hearers. It is not important that hearers remember the content of any particular sermon, but that the sermon empower them to internalize the language and concepts of the faith in such a way that the language and concepts inform who they are, how they ascribe meaning to the world, and how they act and live in the world. To enable this, sermons must be dialogical in nature. This does not mean that preachers must invite oral feedback during every worship service (although this would be refreshing every once in a while). Instead, offering dialogical sermons means that preachers must not hand down absolute, authoritatively pronounced truths; they must offer invitations to the hearers to engage the vision of the sermon intellectually, emotionally, and experientially.

Sermons on the resurrection naturally deal with the broadest and most important aspects of Christian reality and Christian existence because the passion and resurrection of Christ form the center of the Christian story. This is why preachers both more look forward to and are more intimidated by preaching on Easter Sunday than any other day of the liturgical year. But no single sermon can do justice to the full import of the Easter story, nor should preachers try to make one do so. If the sermon is not focused and concrete, the hearers have little chance of engaging and assimilating its vision as their own. Preachers should use the individual gospel narratives that proclaim and interpret the resurrection of Jesus Christ to direct their approaches to the meaning of the resurrection from a single, particular angle. And they must address a single, particular audience in a particular sociohistorical context. Nevertheless, for these focused sermons to possess the potential to be assimilated most effectively by their particular hearers, they must also contain hints at the fuller context of the meaning of the resurrection of Jesus Christ for understanding self, the world, and God; that is, for a Christian approach to reality and existence.

This fuller context of the meaning of the resurrection can be expressed in the following broad definition of resurrection for today's pulpit:

> The proclamation that Jesus Christ is risen from the dead is the central means by which the Christian faith claims that our participation in the meaning of the Christ Event is of Ultimate Significance and thus stretches beyond the finite limits of human existence while wholly participating in that finitude.

The claim that "our participation in the meaning of the Christ Event is of Ultimate Significance and thus stretches beyond the finite limits of human existence" grows out of the assumption that the Easter stories in the four gospels attempt to describe (not define or explain) the ancient church's experience and to claim that Jesus was still present with the disciples and believers after the crucifixion. They describe that somehow the import of Jesus Christ's teachings, miracle stories, acceptance of the marginalized, rituals, and passion was not diminished by his death. To the contrary, the claim that the resurrection effected the exaltation of Jesus to God's right hand (i.e., confirmed Jesus' status as Messiah and/or identified Jesus as divine) implied that the import of and salvation revealed in the Christ Event is eternal.

On the other hand, this eternal quality, this quality of stretching beyond the limits of finite human existence, does not justify interpreting the stories of resurrection in a purely spiritual manner. Were the story of Christ's conquering of death one of spiritual immortality instead of bodily resurrection, the last phrase of our definition, "wholly participating in that finitude," could be omitted. The claim that Jesus Christ was raised in bodily form mythically and metaphorically indicates that the salvation that the Christ Event reveals is a salvation *in* this world, *of* this world. These stories of the physical defeat of the grave are not, as many modern preachers interpret them, an indication that the Christian understanding of salvation is that a person's soul goes to heaven after death. Such a concept was foreign to early Christianity and hinders modern Christians from exploring the call to life now, from applying the good news of Jesus Christ to the struggles and joys of human existence.

Instead of primarily being about immortality, the stories of the resurrection of Jesus Christ testify that Christian existence–life rooted in the story, language, and interpretation of the Christ Event–has a significance that extends beyond the limits that usually define human existence, that is, beyond time, space, and, yes, even death. Human imagination may be able to bring the past (memory) and the future (hope) into the present, but as temporal beings we are not able to exist in more than one dimension of time. Human imagination is also able to bring faraway locations to mind regardless of one's locale, but as physical beings we are not able to be in more than one place at a time. Moreover, human imagination is able to hope that one's identity, self, or soul can continue to exist when one dies; but again, as mortal beings we are not able to achieve immortality.

Humans are only truly transcendent in the sense that we are able to participate in Ultimate Reality (i.e., the eternal, omniscient, omnipotent, omnipresent God). The significance of our existence is thereby extended far beyond the finite limits of our lives. For Christians, Ultimate Reality is described by the story of the Christ Event, along with the biblical history that precedes it and the teachings of the church that follow it. With the story of the resurrection as the penultimate movement in the story of the Christ Event, Christian transcendence is experienced through radical involvement in, commitment to, and love for this finite world and finite existence within the world.

We say that the resurrection is the penultimate movement of the story of the Christ Event as an affirmation of the eschatological character of the Easter stories. At the same time that we must resist the temptation to delay the significance of the salvation described in the story of the resurrection to the afterlife, preachers must also make clear that the meaning of the resurrection is never fully experienced in a single moment, even in a single human lifetime. Eternal, Ultimate, Transcendent Reality (as described in the stories of the resurrection) is by its very nature mysterious, multivalent, and elusive. We participate in the story of the resurrection of Jesus Christ without fully possessing it. We assimilate the story into our worldview without fully defining it. We experience Jesus Christ's resurrection without being able to manipulate or control it. Any time preachers proclaim the Easter story, their role is to offer their congregations a glimpse of a concrete, real aspect of what cannot be seen fully at any one time.

In sum, then, preaching the resurrection of Jesus Christ as described in the Easter stories of the four gospels should not paint a portrait of the past but enable the congregation to develop a new, concrete (albeit incomplete) vision of the present and the future in relation to the experience of Ultimate Meaning in the midst of current reality. And Easter sermons should always contain at least hints of both the present and the future, not one to the complete exclusion of the other. They should show the congregation places where the Eternal God revealed in the risen Christ is present in the midst of everyday life and also that the divine presence is more than the moment of everyday life itself. Preaching the resurrection narratives should make available to the congregation present participation in the Christ Event that in itself points to Ultimate Reality not yet able to be fully experienced in finite existence.

CHAPTER 2

Resurrection in the Gospel of Mark: An Easter Parable

The ending of the Gospel According to Mark is so odd that preachers rarely approach 16:1–8 during the season of Easter.[1] Why would they? There are no resurrection appearances in the garden. There is no appearing behind locked doors. There is no recognition in the breaking of bread. There is no Easter breakfast by the sea. There is no litany of witnesses to the resurrection. There is only an empty tomb about which no one hears:

> When the sabbath was over, Mary Magdalene, and Mary the mother of James, and Salome bought spices, so that they might go and anoint him. And very early on the first day of the week, when the sun had risen, they went to the tomb. They had been saying to one another, "Who will roll away the stone for us from the entrance to the tomb?" When they looked up, they saw that the stone, which was very large, had already been rolled back. As they entered the tomb, they saw a young man, dressed in a white robe, sitting on the right side; and they were alarmed. But he said to them, "Do not be alarmed; you are looking for Jesus of Nazareth, who was crucified. He has been raised; he is not here. Look, there is the place they laid him. But go, tell his disciples

and Peter that he is going ahead of you to Galilee; there
you will see him, just as he told you." So they went out
and fled from the tomb, for terror and amazement had
seized them; and they said nothing to anyone, for they
were afraid. (NRSV)

So why, during the very season that the church celebrates
the resurrection as the center of its faith, would you preach this
story when you have narratives from Matthew, Luke, and John
from which to choose? Why would you preach about an empty
tomb without a risen Christ? Why would you preach about an
unfulfilled command to proclaim Christ as risen?

You would (i.e., you should) do so because in the enigmatic
ending to the second gospel lies the heart of the Easter surprise.
Mark's story of the empty tomb is a reinterpretation of the
message of the resurrection that is as relevant today as it was
for his first-century community. Preachers who are willing to
seek the theological import of the entire gospel as punctuated
with an exclamation point in this enigmatic ending will reap
significant homiletical harvests.

Mark as Parable

Most New Testament scholars agree that although Mark is
the earliest gospel we possess (written around the year 70 C.E.),
it was nevertheless written, as were all the gospels, for a specific
community of faith. In other words, Mark was not published
to introduce people to the story of the Christ Event and establish
a community of faith (i.e., for evangelistic purposes). It was
written for people who had already converted to Christianity,
for Christians who already knew the story of Jesus' life, death,
and resurrection, at least in some form. Therefore, Mark[2] wrote
his narrative for edification purposes—to expand, challenge,
and/or correct the first-century audience's understanding of
various elements and the significance of the Christ Event and
thus to expand, challenge, and/or correct the audience's
understanding of its own Christian existence. Specifically, for
our purposes we can say that since Mark's community knew
something of the story of Jesus, they knew something of the
appearances of the risen Jesus. Thus, the ending of the narrative

can be seen as an intentional riddle of sorts instead of being viewed as incomplete.

Following from this assumption concerning Mark's audience and purpose, we must seek a way of reading Mark as something other than (i.e., more than) biography or history. As Werner Kelber has recognized, the gospel itself offers us an alternative model, that of parable. Adapting C. H. Dodd's classic description of Jesus' parables, we can define a parable as

> a metaphor or simile about the dominion of God that arrests the hearer by its vividness or strangeness and leaves the mind in sufficient doubt about its precise interpretation or application to tease it into active thought to the point of altering one's worldview.[3]

If we look at Mark's version of the parable of the mustard seed in 4:30–32, we can see how parables work in the manner described in this definition:

> With what can we compare the kingdom of God, or what parable will we use for it? It is like a mustard seed, which, when sown upon the ground, is the smallest of all seeds on the earth; yet when it is sown it grows up and becomes the greatest of all shrubs, and puts forth large branches, so that the birds of the air can make nests in its shade. (NRSV)

This brief narrative simile about the dominion of God draws upon something familiar to its original agrarian audience: the planting of a mustard seed. The familiarity of the very small seed, however, quickly gives way to the hyperbolic shrub, which is large enough for birds to nest in its branches. Although a mustard plant could grow into a sizeable herb (a mustard plant usually ranged from two to six feet in height), it is a leafy plant without wooden branches large enough or strong enough to support birds' nests. This odd twist in the parable is indeed the very hinge on which any interpretation must swing. To understand what the dominion of God is *like,* one must tease out the significance of the exaggeration. In what way is God's dominion like something that grows beyond its expected capacity in order to function in a manner outside its usual ability and involve those not normally included? Parables teach us and shape our worldviews by indirectly raising questions about our current understanding of that which is Ultimate.

If we apply this definition of parables not only to short narratives spoken by Jesus but to Mark's entire narrative about Jesus, the odd ending (16:1–8) makes sense. It makes sense not as a literal account of the conclusion of the Christ Event, but as a literary-theological technique used to call the readers' minds into sufficient doubt about the precise interpretation of the resurrection and indeed of the whole of the Christ Event.

The result of struggling with the interpretation of Mark's Easter story and of the gospel narrative as a whole will alter the worldview of his Christian audience and the readers' questioning of their relationship to the Christ Event. This is made clear in chapter 4, where Mark collects most of Jesus' parables that he includes in the gospel. In verses 10–12 the author presents the disciples as asking Jesus why he speaks in parables. Jesus responds:

> "To you has been given the secret [or mystery, Gk. *mysterion*] of the kingdom of God, but for those outside, everything comes in parables; in order that
>> 'they may indeed look, but
>>> not perceive,
>> and may indeed listen, but
>>> not understand;
>> so that they may not turn
>>> again and be forgiven.'"
>
> (4:11–12, NRSV; the scripture quote is adapted from Isa. 6:9–10)

For Mark, parables divide characters in the narrative between dominion insiders and outsiders. Parables illuminate the mystery of God's dominion for those who are inside God's dominion, but for those outside they lead to misperception, misunderstanding, and lack of repentance. Therefore, it is appropriate to read the entire parabolic narrative of Mark as dividing the readers into insiders and outsiders. The question that remains to be examined is what criterion Mark uses to make this division.

The Son of God

The opening verse of Mark reads: "The beginning of the good news of Jesus Christ, the Son of God" (1:1). Instead of seeing in this line the opening of the first passage or even the first section of Mark, the incomplete sentence should be recognized as the title for the entire narrative. As the original title to the gospel, the line places a couple of important pieces of the parabolic puzzle together quickly. First, because the *entire* narrative is "the beginning," we should not be surprised by the open-endedness of 16:1–8. Mark does not claim to be telling the whole story of the Christ Event, only its *beginning.* The rest of the story (i.e., the post–empty tomb story) is assumed, implied, or yet to be completed. Second, the writing is not just telling a story about Jesus' life and death; it is defining Jesus *as* the Messiah and the Son of God. It describes in what way Jesus is to be understood as Christ and as the Son of God.[4] Thus, Mark is narrative christology attempting to correct, challenge, and/or expand the readers' christology. A proper understanding of Jesus Christ as the Son of God is the criterion by which dominion insiders are distinguished from outsiders.

The significance of Jesus as the Son of God quickly shows up again in Jesus' baptism, the first scene in which Jesus appears in the gospel:

And just as he was coming up out of the water, he saw the heavens torn apart and the Spirit descending like a dove on him. And a voice came from heaven, "You are my Son, the Beloved; with you I am well pleased." (1:10–11, NRSV)

Unlike Matthew and Luke, in which Jesus is pronounced the Son of God at birth, Mark presents God claiming Jesus as the Messiah at the baptism. *Messiah* (Hebrew) and *Christ* (Greek) mean "anointed one." In Mark the baptism is the point at which Jesus is anointed and becomes the Son of God. It is important to recognize that in Mark this "messiahing" is a private epiphany for Jesus. The voice addresses Jesus directly in second-person speech ("*You* are my son"), while in Matthew's version of the baptism the heavenly voice seems to be revealing Jesus' identity (already established at birth) to the crowd in third-person speech ("*This* is my Son," Mt. 3:17). This scene is the first indication that Mark's gospel is a thoroughly ironic narrative in the sense that readers are in a privileged position, knowing Jesus' identity before characters in the story (except Jesus) do. This will allow the readers to evaluate which of the characters are insiders and which are not, and therefore to choose the proper characters with whom they should identify.

Following his baptism and temptation, Mark offers a summary of Jesus' proclamation (and therefore a summary of the theme of the Markan narrative): "The time is fulfilled, and the kingdom of God has come near; repent, and believe in the good news" (1:15). The use of "good news" recalls the title (1:1) and indicates that the good news of the arrival of the dominion of God and the good news of Jesus Christ as the Son of God are the same. Therefore, those who repent and believe in the good news are inside the dominion of God when they understand Jesus to be the Son of God *in the same manner* that Mark interprets Jesus' identity as God's Son.

Immediately after summarizing Jesus' teaching, Mark presents Jesus as calling his first disciples in 1:16–20. It is a brief, straightforward scene. Jesus' presumably first words to Simon, Andrew, James, and John are "Follow me." Although we are given no indication that Mark presents them as having known anything about Jesus prior to this encounter, they respond obediently without hesitation. They leave livelihood and family to be with Jesus. Even though they were not at the baptism, they appear at first glance to recognize Jesus clearly. Indeed, in conjunction with readers' natural predisposition to identify with the disciples as founders of the postresurrection church (presuming this is part of their shared tradition), the disciples' quick and obedient response to Jesus' call invites readers to identify with them and accept them as their representatives in the narrative.

And the choice seems to be a good one because everyone else who encounters Jesus in Galilee (with the exception of the demons) does not recognize him. This is evidenced by the fact that some respond with amazement to his miracles and the authority of his teaching (one should not be surprised that the Son of God has such power and authority) and others oppose him. The fact that Jesus' significance could not yet be understood by those other characters in the story is evident in the so-called Messianic Secret, Jesus' repetitious silencing of those he encounters (1:25, 34, 43–44; 3:12; 5:43; 7:36; 8:26). The problem for the readers is that, as the narrative progresses, the disciples, with whom the readers have identified, seem more and more to join the company of outsiders, those who do not recognize Jesus' identity. As already noted, Jesus speaks in parables in chapter 4, and dominion insiders should understand them and recognize the mystery to which they point. But the disciples do *not* understand the parables. Jesus must interpret his first parable (the parable of the sower) for them and asks, "Do you not understand this parable? Then how will you understand all the parables?" (4:13). Moreover, after Jesus has spoken his last parable in chapter 4, the narrator notes that Jesus had to explain all of them to his disciples in private (4:34).

In the very next scene, Jesus stills a storm at the disciples' request, and the scene ends on a bad note for the disciples:

> He [Jesus] said to them, "Why are you afraid? Have you still no faith?" And they were filled with great awe and said to one another, "Who then is this that even the wind and the sea obey?" (4:40–41)

Like the crowds, the disciples are filled with fear and amazement, and from their own mouths the readers hear that Jesus' closest companions do not know who Jesus really is!

The misunderstanding of the ones with whom the readers have identified forces the readers to begin to question their own understandings of Jesus. In a very short narrative space, Mark has bombarded the readers with a reversal of the initial impression of the disciples. It is important to remember that Mark is writing a parable and not necessarily trying to paint a negative historical picture of the disciples. As characters with whom the readers have been invited to identify, the disciples are characterized in this manner to serve the purpose of inviting the readers to question their own understandings of Jesus and of God's dominion.

But Mark's indictment of the disciples (and of the readers) is far from complete. After Jesus walks on water, the disciples are amazed and fearful and do not understand Jesus' words

(7:17–23; see also 6:52). After feeding the four thousand, Jesus warns the disciples of "the leaven of the Pharisees and the leaven of Herod" (8:15). They, however, confuse the miracle with the teaching and evoke from Jesus a rebuke that recalls the fact that parables hide the mystery of the dominion of God from those outside: "Why are you talking about having no bread? Do you still not perceive or understand? Are your hearts hardened? Do you have eyes, and fail to see? Do you have ears, and fail to hear?" (8:17–18).

There are two peaks in the narrative at which the disciples' misunderstanding reaches its highest points. The lower of those two peaks comes at the midpoint of the plotline, marking the transition from Jesus' ministry in Galilee (1:14–8:26) to his being on the way to Jerusalem (8:27–10:52). In this introductory scene (8:27–9:1), which sets much of the tone for the travel narrative, Jesus asks the disciples who "people" claim he is. The people do not know and have been guessing incorrectly that Jesus is John the Baptist, Elijah, or one of the prophets. (This answer recalls the confusion about Jesus described in 6:14–16.) When Jesus asks the disciples who *they* think he is, Peter speaks up as the representative disciple with the answer for which the readers are hoping: "You are the Messiah." But the answer Peter and the readers assume to be correct is met with the same silencing that Jesus commands of others: "And he sternly ordered them not to tell anyone about him." Jesus then goes on to describe, for the first time, his passion and resurrection. At this point it becomes clear that Peter's answer did not reveal a proper understanding of Jesus' identity and mission, for he rebukes Jesus for saying that he must die. Jesus rebukes Peter yet again, identifying him with Satan. He then describes true disciples as those who are willing to die for the sake of the good news, which, as we have seen, is the news of the arrival of the dominion of God and of the fact that Jesus is the Son of God.

Immediately following this peak of misunderstanding, the disciples receive a revelation that allows them a chance to see inside the mystery of the dominion of God: the transfiguration (9:2–13). Jesus takes Peter, James, and John up a mountain where his appearance is transfigured and Moses and Elijah appear. Such a vision should have been enough to make the disciples realize Jesus' true identity. But Peter, speaking out of fear, suggests building tents and remaining on the mountain, a signal that they do not yet understand that Jesus' role as Son of God must be fulfilled in Jerusalem. But then a voice from heaven speaks to the disciples: "This is my Son, the Beloved, listen to him!" Instead of a private epiphany for Jesus such as occurred at his baptism, the second time Jesus is called God's Son within the narrative is for the sake of the disciples. But by Jesus' instructing them, as he had instructed so many before, to tell no one what they had seen, the narrator lets us know that the disciples still do not understand the significance of what is happening before their very eyes nor the significance of the One right before them. But for the first time, Jesus' words give us a clue as to what it will take for them to understand. Jesus instructs them to tell no one about the transfiguration "until after the Son of Man had risen from the dead." Now the readers suspect that the disciples will continue as outsiders until the end of the narrative. At that point, full understanding should be achieved.

In line with the expectation, the disciples appear to be further and further outside the dominion of God as the plot progresses and Jesus continues to head toward Jerusalem, presumably allowing for greater repentance at the end. Jesus predicts his passion and resurrection two more times. Each time the disciples respond inappropriately, indicating that they do not understand the significance of Jesus' words. In the first instance, immediately after Jesus tells them of his suffering, they respond by arguing about which of them is the greatest (9:30–37). In the second, James and John (who had been on the Mountain of Transfiguration) respond by asking of Jesus the favor of appointing them to sit as his right and left hands when he enters his glory (10:32–45).

The disciples look no better to the readers once the narrative moves into Jerusalem (11:1–15:47). And indeed the irony that characterizes Mark's narrative becomes thickest at this point. Actions and speeches point to Jesus' true identity and mission in ways that are recognized by the readers but not by those acting and speaking in the narrative. Indeed, much of the Jerusalem narrative is flavored by the theme of an ironic, paradoxical coronation ceremony in which Jesus is enthroned as the messianic Son of God, but no one in the story (except Jesus) realizes it:

- Jesus enters the city in a parade where he is declared the one coming in the name of Lord, the one who will bring about the kingdom of David (11:1–10). But when he enters the temple, no ceremony takes place: Jesus looks around and then leaves (11:11).

- Jesus is anointed, not by the high priest in the temple, but by a woman in the house of a leper. Moreover, the anointing is criticized for its extravagance (14:3–9).

- The farewell meal, where Jesus foretells Judas' betrayal, alludes to his death in the Lord's Supper, and foretells the desertion of the disciples and denial by Peter, is the messianic banquet of the one being crowned (14:17–31).

- Jesus does appear before the high priest, but not to be anointed or crowned. He is tried by the Sanhedrin (14:53–65).

- Likewise, Jesus enters the palace, but not to take up residence. He is tried by Pilate. Instead of shouting praises to him, as the people would at a coronation (and as they did when he entered the city), the crowd calls for his crucifixion (15:1–15).

- As they lead him off to be crucified, the guards robe and crown Jesus in mockery (15:16–20).

- When Jesus is crucified, a sign is placed over his head that reads "The King of the Jews" (15:26). If this were not enough to let the readers know that the cross is Jesus' throne, in the next line the narrator notes that two bandits are hanging on his left and his right (15:27), recalling Jesus' conversation with James and John concerning their request to sit on his right and left when he was in his glory. Jesus' answer included the words, "To sit at my right hand or at my left hand is not mine to grant, but it is for those for whom it has been prepared" (10:40). The cross is Jesus' glory!

Not only do Jesus' opponents not recognize the very coronation happening in their midst, but the disciples' misunderstanding increases as well. Judas betrays Jesus (14:10–11, 43–45); Peter, James, and John fall asleep when Jesus asks them to keep watch while he prays about his coming death (14:32–41); all the disciples flee when Jesus is arrested (14:50–52), even though they had said they would die before deserting Jesus (14:31); and Peter denies Jesus three times as predicted (14:66–72). The last time Peter denies Jesus he uses the words, "I do not know this man you are talking about." He thinks he is lying, but the readers know he ironically speaks the truth: He truly does *not* know Jesus the Messiah, Son of God.

At the very point where the disciples' status as dominion outsiders is most pronounced and they have all left the narrative, the readers finally come upon a human character who recognizes Jesus' true identity. At the moment Jesus breathes his last, not some religious leader, not some disciple, but the very Gentile centurion who oversees his execution says, "Truly this man was God's Son!" (15:39). The character with whom the Christian audience would be least likely to identify with utters the only human confession to parallel the heavenly voice at Jesus' baptism and transfiguration. The type of character expected to be farthest away from the dominion of God is the only one who stands inside God's dominion, because he alone has experienced the full revelatory power of the cross. Recognizing the crucifixion as the moment in which Jesus' identity is defined for the Christian faith is the criterion by which Mark divides dominion insiders and outsiders.

What are the readers to make of the parabolic ending at the empty tomb once this is realized?

The Empty Tomb

The Burial

As we return now to look closely at Mark 16:1–8, the parabolic ending to a parabolic narrative, we must first see how Mark connects the closing scene at the empty tomb to the scene at the cross. Following the climactic, if ironic, exclamation of the centurion at Jesus' death, Joseph of Arimathea asks Pilate for Jesus' body so that he may bury it (15:42–47). Joseph's characterization and actions have long been misunderstood by interpreters. Mark tells us that he is a "respected member of the council" (i.e., Sanhedrin) and that he is "waiting expectantly for the kingdom of God" (v. 43). Although these phrases may have a positive ring to them, they are negative in the context of Mark's larger narrative. First, one who is a respected member of the council is not meant to be respected by Mark's readers. In the trial scene the narrator explicitly states that *all* the chief priests, elders, and scribes were assembled and that they *all* condemned Jesus (14:64). Second, in 1:15 the summary of Jesus' message is that the dominion of God has already come near. The reader is meant to recognize that it has come near in Jesus himself as the Son of God. Immediately after Jesus' death–the point at which Jesus' identity is most clearly revealed–Joseph is described as someone *still awaiting* the arrival of God's dominion.

Interpreters have usually viewed Joseph in a positive light (indeed he is regarded as the patron saint of funeral directors), but Mark presents him in a very negative fashion. This means that we should expect his burial of Jesus not to be a burial of honor, but a negative action that proceeds from a negative character. And indeed the burial is the final insult made by those who condemned and executed Jesus. Mark's note that evening had arrived and the Sabbath was beginning is a signal to the readers that Joseph's concern was not for Jesus but for the Sabbath. We must remember that Jesus has disputed with Jewish leaders like Joseph concerning honoring the Sabbath (e.g., 2:23–28; 3:1–6). Indeed, Joseph's desire to bury Jesus before the Sabbath clearly implies he has not accepted Jesus' statement that the Son of man is Lord of the Sabbath (2:28).

The manner in which Joseph buries Jesus is described briefly but with enough detail to indicate its impropriety. He buys a linen cloth, takes the body down from the cross and wraps it in the linen cloth, lays the body in the tomb, and rolls a stone in front of the door of the tomb (15:46). The narrator ends the scene by noting that two of the women who watched the crucifixion from afar (Mary Magdalene and Mary, Jesus' mother [who in Mark 15–16 is curiously identified as the mother of Jesus' various brothers but not explicitly as Jesus' mother; compare 6:3]) see where the body is laid (15:47). By implication, they have watched the manner in which Joseph has buried Jesus and recognize that it is incomplete. There is no preparation of the body for burial, no anointing. Instead the corpse is quickly wrapped up and tossed in the tomb. Out of sight, out of mind. It is this disrespectful incompleteness that sets the stage for the women's actions in 16:1–8.

The Final Epiphany

The closing scene opens with an odd time reference (16:1). The three women who had watched the crucifixion from afar (Mary Magdalene, Mary [Jesus' mother], and Salome) wait until the Sabbath is over to buy spices to anoint Jesus' body. This description nonsensically implies that they are shopping after sundown on Saturday night (Jewish days begin at sundown instead of sunrise). Instead of looking for some historical explanation like a late-night Mediterranean convenience store, we should recognize Mark's parabolic techniques by now. Although they wish to offer Jesus respect, similar to Joseph, they are being portrayed as having honored the Sabbath before honoring the Lord of the Sabbath. Their delay in shopping for spices shows that they do not fully understand Jesus' identity.

But were not these three women described by Mark as having followed Jesus, having provided for him in Galilee, and with other women having come up to Jerusalem with him? More importantly, were these not the three women present at the crucifixion when all the disciples betrayed, scattered, and/ or denied Jesus (15:40–41)? Yes, but Mark also specifically mentions that they were watching the crucifixion "from a distance" (Gk. *apo makrothen*). This watching Jesus die from afar, in contrast to the centurion's location right beside Jesus, allows for Mark's ambiguous characterization of the women. They have not run away in the manner that the men did, but neither have they denied themselves and taken up their own crosses in their following of Jesus (8:34–35). They watch from a safe distance and save their own lives. Thus, although the women alone remain to come to the tomb, we should not expect them to be glowing examples of true discipleship in this final scene.

If this interpretation of the women is not yet convincing, one must only consider that in addition to honoring the Sabbath, early the next morning (i.e., Sunday morning) the women come to the tomb *to anoint Jesus' body* (16:1). If they came up to Jerusalem with Jesus (15:41), then surely the readers are to suppose that they knew of the promises that Jesus made along the way to Jerusalem, that after his death he would be raised (8:31; 9:31; 10:34). But they assume him to be dead. They expect to find a body lying in the tomb in need of the completion of the burial ritual. Moreover, should they not have remembered that when the woman anointed Jesus in Bethany, Jesus claimed that she had anointed his body beforehand for its burial (Gk. *proelaben myrisai to soma mou eis ton entaphiasmon,* 14:8)?

But the three women express no concern that their trek to the tomb might be futile because Jesus might have been raised, nor that their anointing will duplicate something already done. Their only concern is with the stone (16:3). They saw Joseph roll it in place (15:46–47), assume that it is still in place, and now, just before the tomb comes into sight, question who they might find to roll it away again. If Mark were trying to present a historical picture, we would expect him to explain why the women hadn't thought of this before they were on the way to the tomb. Did they really hope to find someone strong enough to roll away a tombstone sitting around in the cemetery just after dawn on Sunday morning? But Mark is not recording history. He is writing a dramatic parable. All the details need not make perfect historical sense in order to make theological sense.

As soon as the women utter their concerns about the stone, they arrive at the tomb, look up, and see that the stone has already been rolled away (16:4). Mark, like the other evangelists, leaves many details unexplained. How was Jesus raised? When was Jesus resurrected—as soon as sundown occurred on "the third day," sometime during the night, or just moments before the women arrived on Sunday morning? How was the stone rolled away? Who rolled it away? Was it rolled away to let Jesus out or just to let the women in? Again, to ask such questions of Mark's narrative is to ignore its parabolic, literary nature. The plot demands that the stone must be rolled away so that the women may enter the tomb, encounter the young man, and see that the tomb is empty; and thus Mark has it rolled away.

Mark's choice of wording for the women's "looking up" to see that the door of the tomb is open clues the readers in to the fact that what has occurred (the stone's being rolled away) and what is about to occur (the encounter with the young man) are miraculous in nature. Even though the Greek word for "look up" (*anablepo*) can literally mean looking in an upward direction, in Mark the word appears only in miraculous settings. When he feeds the crowd (6:41) and when he heals the deaf and dumb man (7:34), Jesus "looks up" to heaven in prayer. Moreover, in Mark's two stories of Jesus' healing blind men (8:24 and 10:51–52), their regaining of sight is described with this term. These healing scenes, being narrated just before major narrative transition points (Peter's confession at Caesarea Philippi and Jesus' first passion prediction [8:27–33] and the entry into Jerusalem [11:1–11]), are often interpreted as symbolic passages referring to the overcoming of the blindness of those who misunderstood Jesus' identity. In the first healing (8:22–26), at the end of the Galilean ministry, the blind man regains sight only in stages, reflecting perhaps the disciples' slowness to see Jesus' true identity. In the second scene (10:46–52), the healed man "follows" Jesus on his "way" (10:52), a verbal indicator of true discipleship recalling Jesus' command to take up one's cross and follow (8:34; see also the references to Jesus' being "on the way" [Gk. *hodos*] to Jerusalem [9:33–34; 10:17, 32, 46]. Note: The NRSV is unhelpful in that it translates *hodos* several different ways in these verses.).

Thus, the readers might expect the miraculous empty tomb to be eye-opening for the three women and might reveal to them Jesus' true identity. And indeed language of "seeing" appears in all of verses 4–7. In addition to "looking up," the women "see" (Gk. *theoreo*) the stone rolled away in verse 4. (*Theoreo* appears in many settings without significance, but it should be noted that it also appears in 15:40 to describe the women watching the crucifixion.) In verse 5 the women "see" (Gk. *horao*) the young man. In verse 6 the young man tells the women to "look" (Gk. *ide*) where Jesus' body had been lying. And, finally, in verse 7 the young man instructs the women to tell the disciples and Peter that they will "see" (Gk. *horao*) Jesus in Galilee. But all this "seeing" is ironic. At the end of the scene the women clearly still do not *see* Jesus in his full identity as the Son of God.

When the women enter the tomb (v. 5), they find it empty, at least to the extent that Jesus' corpse is not in it. There is, however, a young man (Gk. *neaniskos*) sitting to the right side of the tomb. Although this is a miraculous encounter, Mark's story should not be harmonized with Matthew's version of the empty tomb, in which case the young man would be assumed to be an angel. Mark's choice of wording is careful. Indeed, the readers have met this young man before. When Jesus is arrested, with him and the disciples in the garden is a young man (Gk. *neaniskos*) who attempts to follow the arrested Jesus after the others have scattered (14:51–52). The young man is mentioned out of the blue without any attempt to identify him. He is described only in terms of what he is wearing...or not wearing. As he follows (Gk. *synakoloutheo*), he is wearing only a linen cloth (Gk. *sindon*), which foreshadows Joseph's wrapping Jesus in a linen cloth (Gk. *sindon*) at the rushed burial (15:46). But the guards attempt to seize him, and he is forced to flee naked. Now he reappears in the empty tomb and is re-dressed in a white robe (Gk. *stolen leyken*), which recalls Jesus' exceedingly white (Gk. *leyka lian*) garments at the transfiguration (9:3).

Markan scholars have offered many different historical and literary interpretations of the young man's role and identity in the gospel. And indeed, in a reading of Mark as parabolic, his appearance must be considered key. His clothes parallel the "clothes" of Jesus' death (linen) and self-revelatory glory (white). In other words, he seems to model a participation in and identification with the death and resurrection. We shall understand the significance of this when we have reached the end of 16:1–8.

The connection between this scene and the stories of the transfiguration and the arrest in the garden deepens. The women's emotional response to the sight of the young man is to be "alarmed" (Gk. *ekthambeo*, 16:5–6). This Greek word appears only two other times in the gospel of Mark. (In attempting to draw out the appropriate nuance in each of Mark's uses of *ekthambeo,* the NRSV offers three different translations of the term and inadvertently disguises the repetition from the

English reader.) First, when Jesus comes down from the mountain after having been transfigured and declared the Son of God by the heavenly voice, the great crowd at the bottom is "overcome with awe" (9:15). Second, when Jesus takes the inner circle of disciples with him in Gethsemane to pray before his arrest, he becomes "distressed" (14:33). In addition to helping the readers connect the young man at the tomb with the one in Gethsemane, the use of this word indicates that the scene is an epiphany much like the transfiguration and that the young man is the instrument of that epiphany.

When the young man speaks (16:6), he first attempts to comfort the women: "Do not be alarmed" (Gk. *me ekthambeisthe*). He then offers two declarative statements: "You are looking for Jesus of Nazareth, who was crucified. He has been raised; he is not here." The juxtaposition in these statements is significant. On the one hand, it points to the vast distance between the women's expectations concerning Jesus and the present reality of Jesus. The fact that they expect the Crucified One's body to be found in a tomb reveals that they do not fully understand the crucifixion they witnessed from a distance. On the other hand, it makes clear that while Mark 16:1–8 is a parabolic, open ending, it is not a failed ending. While the risen Jesus does not appear in Mark as he does in the other gospels, Jesus is clearly presented as having been resurrected from the dead in accordance with his own predictions (8:31; 9:31; 10:34). For Mark, Jesus is emphatically the risen Son of God, just as he is the crucified Son of God. But he is also the hide-and-seek Son of God, who has not yet been truly seen by the disciples or the women.

But the young man offers them the opportunity to see. Mark's wording at this point is precise: "But go, tell his disciples and Peter that he is going ahead of you to Galilee; there you will see him, just as he told you" (16:7). "But" (Gk. *alla*) indicates a contrast. Now the women can only see the empty place where Jesus' body was once lying, but they *will* see Jesus himself in Galilee.

The mentioning of the disciples *and Peter* recalls the deserting by all, but especially the denial by Peter. Thus, the resurrection appearance in Galilee is to be redemptive. Those who did not know Jesus will finally know him fully, as was expected by readers following the transfiguration when Jesus instructed Peter, James, and John to tell no one about what had occurred until after the resurrection (9:9).

The young man's statement that the risen Jesus has gone before them to Galilee (Gk. *proagei hymas eis ten Galilaian*) just as Jesus had said echoes back to 14:28, where Jesus has just predicted the scattering of the disciples and then promises to go before them into Galilee after the resurrection (Gk. *alla meta to egerthenai me proaxo hymas eis ten Galilaian*). Attached to this statement expressed in the present tense is a promise expressed in the future tense: "There you will see him" (Gk. *ekei auton opsesthe*). The fact that this promise is emphatically stated—"you *will* see him," not "you *can* or *might* see him"—and reiterated but is not fulfilled within the narrative allows for the readers' knowledge of the tradition that Jesus appeared to the disciples to remain intact, while at the same time using the promise in a parabolic fashion. Mark must mean something more than that the disciples and Peter and these three women literally saw the risen Jesus in Galilee.

Parabolic Silence

The problem, of course, is that the women do not follow the instructions of the young man (16:8). They do not go to Galilee to meet the risen Son of God. They do not tell the disciples of the epiphany at the tomb. Using a strong double negative, the narrator says that the women said nothing to no one (Gk. *oudeni ouden eipan*). Like the crowds and disciples before the crucifixion, the women are filled with terror, amazement, and fear—all Markan signals of misunderstanding and unfaithfulness. Any hope that the ambiguous characterization of the women would take a positive turn dies with the end of the story.

But the hope of seeing the risen Jesus does not. Indeed, this odd ending of Mark's gospel is clearly not meant to draw to a close the readers' experience of the narrative. After all, 16:1–8 is simply the end of the *beginning* of the good news of Jesus Christ, Son of God (1:1). Moreover, as a parable the strange and vivid ending sends the readers into a tailspin of doubt about the gospel's precise interpretation, teasing their minds into active thought with the potential of altering their understandings of the Christ Event and their relationships to it.

If Mark is primarily narrative christology, specifically defining in what way Jesus is the Messiah, the Son of God, then it seems clear that it is the cross, not the resurrection, that Mark interprets as most clearly revealing the true nature of Jesus' identity. One cannot help but wonder whether Mark's community has emphasized the reverse, and thus the second gospel serves as a corrective to the community theology. Again, Mark has not done away with the resurrection, but he has removed it from sight so that it must be reinterpreted in light of the cross.

Of course, Mark's readers were invited to identify with the disciples and thus to hear themselves being indicted as those who have abandoned the cross. However, unlike the disciples who, in the narrative, never receive word of the resurrection, the readers have heard the testimonies of both the centurion at the cross and the young man at the empty tomb. This means that Mark's use of irony has been employed so that the entire gospel might be read as a call story, inviting the readers to discipleship that embraces the cross and participates in faithful suffering, inviting the readers to repent in a way the disciples and the women never do. In place of the failure of the male disciples (desertion and denial), and of the three women (fearful silence), the readers are called by Mark's ending to meet the risen Jesus and to lead others to do the same. But how are readers to do this?

In the gospel, foreshadowing indicates that the encounter with the resurrected Jesus takes place in Galilee. Clearly, in Mark's parabolic world, Galilee plays a role more symbolic than literal or geographical. Galilee is the place where Jesus turned the world on its head, raising questions about who is inside and who is outside the dominion of God. Galilee is the place where Jesus ate with sinners, healed the sick, fed the hungry crowds, broke the Sabbath laws, and taught with authority about God's dominion. Mark invites his readers to recognize that it is in such settings, when such activities are taking place, that we meet the risen Son of God, who gave his life as a ransom for our sins (10:45). In other words, Mark not only places the resurrection in the shadow of the cross, he hides the story of the disciples' historic seeing of the resurrected Jesus in the shadow of the readers' experience of the crucified and risen Jesus. For Mark, celebrating the resurrection as a past victory over the tomb misses the point. Celebrating it as a current experience of those living out the meaning of the cross in active participation in Jesus Christ's ministry in the world is the point. Indeed, it is the point of *entry* into the dominion of God. This is the continuation of the good news of Jesus Christ, Son of God (cf. 1:1).

As with all parables, Mark's ending (and the entire gospel) is multivalent and can be interpreted in many valid ways. The task of preaching Mark 16:1–8 is, in the context of a single sermon, to offer one such interpretation without being dogmatic in a way that closes off other interpretations. The preacher must indicate a way that the incomplete narrative denouement can be resolved in the life of the congregation. She or he must offer the congregation directions to meet in their lives and their world the risen Jesus Christ who is never met in the narrative.

In essence, the preacher must lead the congregation through the homiletical experience of having identified with the disciples to identifying with the young man at the empty tomb. The young man, who was with the disciples, fled naked when Jesus was led away to the cross, but returned, clothed in glory and speaking of Jesus' resurrection afterward. The young man represents the very repentance called for in the summary of Jesus' proclamation: "The time is fulfilled, and the kingdom of God has come near; repent, and believe in the good news" (1:15).

The preacher, however, is well advised to follow Mark's example and resist the temptation to chastise the congregation for emphasizing the resurrection while missing the point of the cross. On Easter Sunday, too many preachers offer a backhanded welcome to those who were not in worship on Good Friday (or perhaps any other time of the year but Christmas Eve). By contrast, Mark's parabolic approach is indirect and inductive. Instead of shaking his finger at his readers for misinterpreting Jesus a in way that is more comfortable (i.e., avoiding the cross and its implications for discipleship), Mark invites the readers on a narrative journey—through Galilee to Jerusalem and back again to Galilee—that results in self-indictment and repentance. Mark is not trying to invoke guilt, but to offer a new vision of the Christ Event that in turn leads to a new self-understanding of discipleship. And that is no mean goal for contemporary proclamation on the resurrection of Jesus Christ.

Mark's Stained-Glass Window (Mk. 16:1—8)[5]■

The year was 1899. I was only about eight years old, and for a while everyone had been talking about the turn of the century: "the twentieth century this" and "the twentieth century that." More than anything, people in Tinyville, Mississippi—the town where I grew up—thought God was going to do something new and exciting in the next century. I don't know, I guess we just thought God had a thing for round numbers or something.

Some people started saying that God had chosen the twentieth century for the time when Christ would return to earth. They thought this was confirmed by the fact that a northern magazine had recently just started up that was called *The Christian Century.* I mean, if Yankees could even recognize it, it had to be true. Soon the word had spread like wildfire and the whole town had become convinced that Christ was coming back during the twentieth century.

You see, there's not a lot to talk about in a small town like Tinyville. Oh, everybody talked. Old men playing pinochle down at the hardware store talked. Women at the quilting bee talked. Businessmen talked over coffee at Bonnie's Diner at 10:30 every morning. But they usually didn't talk *about* anything. They just chatted the smallest small town talk a small town could talk.

So when something new like Christ's second coming came up, everybody got excited. After all, the turn of the century only comes around every hundred years or so and the end of the world even less than that—you just can't let something like that pass by without comment. So everybody was talking about it, and it didn't take long for everybody to agree that Christ was indeed packing his heavenly bags and would soon be arriving back on earth.

But agreement about Christ's return didn't end the discussion. It just gave way to hordes of speculation about the details of the divine visitation. When? Where? How would Christ return?

Now there was one man in town–Mr. Romano–who didn't believe Christ was going to return in the twentieth century, which was no great surprise to the people of Tinyville because everyone knew Mr. Romano didn't believe in Christ. He didn't believe in God. He didn't believe in anything. If Mr. Romano hadn't lived in Tinyville, no one except the librarian would have known what the word *atheist* meant. In fact, if he hadn't lived there, no one would have known what the word *cynic* meant. To this day, I'm not sure if Mr. Romano was a cynic because he didn't believe in God, or if he was an atheist because he was so cynical; but I am sure he was the meanest man I ever knew as a young boy.

All the kids in town knew where Mr. Romano lived. His little, brown house was surrounded by big leafy trees that made the house always seem dark, even on the brightest of days. All the kids believed that if you went into his yard, you'd get invited into dinner and, of course, *you* would be the main course. If for some reason, he couldn't catch you, he'd just spit on you, and warts would grow all over your body. He was nasty. At least, that was the reputation he had among us kids.

But not only among children. Adults also held Mr. Romano in low esteem. Every so often, someone would mention him at church and say that we needed to pray for his sinful, soon-to-be-burning-in-hell soul. And no one ever spoke well of him, in or out of church.

Well, that's not completely true. There was one thing about Mr. Romano that everyone admired. He was a photographer, and everyone admitted that he was a good one. Cameras were few and far-between back then. They were expensive and, as wonderful as they were, the pictures they took weren't that great. But if a picture is worth a thousand words, Mr. Romano's photos were worth a million words set to music. So the town tolerated his cynicism and his atheism, just so there'd be someone around to take pictures of the mayor, and of weddings and family reunions, and of newborn babies. But otherwise, no one made an effort to socialize with him, to be friendly with him on the street, or even to talk with him. And, for the most part, that was just fine with Mr. Romano.

But when everybody started agreeing that Jesus was on his way back, Mr. Romano started pushing his way into conversations all over the place. He constantly mocked the town for its religious fervor: "You think Christ is going to return? That's the silliest thing I've ever heard. How can you think someone's coming back when he never came the first time?! You people will believe anything! Just look around the world— does this look like some place that God has redeemed? I'll believe Christ is coming back when I see it with my own eyes, not before."

But in spite of Mr. Romano's mockery, everyone else in town believed it: The turn of the century would mark the return of Christ. In fact, Tinyvillians were so convinced that Christ was coming back that what occupied most of the discussion was the question of *when* Christ would make his way to *Tinyville.*

I remember at the dinner table one Sunday after church— we went to Resurrection Methodist Episcopal Church, South— Daddy started telling Mama that the men's Sunday school class that morning had been discussing that maybe the church should try to find a way to attract Christ to choose Tinyville as the town he came to first. I asked Daddy why anybody, much less Jesus, would want to come to Tinyville. After Mama said her usual, "Jackson Lewis Hillman, children are meant to be seen and not heard," Daddy said, "Actually, Jackson's point is well taken, Mother. There isn't anything here to attract Jesus. We need to 'holify' our town somehow, so that Jesus will choose us. Just think of the prestige of being the town where Jesus' cloud lands on that great day. Tinyville wouldn't be a no-name town anymore. It would become the holiest of the holy sites. Just think of all the tourists who would come here!"

I don't guess any of us realized that if Christ had returned, there would no longer be any "here" for tourists to come to, because that's what the whole town started focusing on: getting

Jesus to Tinyville. The editor of the local newspaper, *The Tinyville World Scope,* was a member of Daddy's Sunday school class and decided to run a contest where everyone could submit ideas for attracting Jesus to Tinyville. The person with the best idea would win a lifetime subscription to the paper, which didn't seem like too much of a sacrifice to the editor, since he assumed Christ would be returning any day now.

All kinds of suggestions were submitted. Somebody suggested that the entire town do something biblical like wiping sheep's blood on their doorposts, but it was quickly pointed out that that ritual would make Jesus pass over the town. Miss Bonnie, over at the diner, said we should change the name of the town from Tinyville to New Jerusalem, Mississippi. A lot of people liked that idea at first, but overall it was decided that it was a little too presumptuous. I mean what if Jesus came back somewhere else, like Jacksonville, first and *it* became the New Jerusalem. Then there'd be two New Jerusalems in Mississippi, and we'd be the old New Jerusalem and might be forced to go back to being plain old Tinyville. It just didn't seem worth all the trouble and potential embarrassment.

The idea that won was that the whole town should come together to put a new stained-glass window in Resurrection Methodist Church's sanctuary—not just any stained glass window, but the brightest, most colorful, most spectacular stained-glass window ever seen. But even more than that it must be different than any other stained-glass window that had ever existed before—something appropriate for a new century in which Christ would change everything. So the window itself should somehow be able to change.

The town all jumped on the idea and decided that what they needed was a foreign artist to design the window for them. So they brought someone in all the way from California. And this is what he came up with: He designed a square window with square panels that moved along grooves—you know, like those children's puzzles where you move the squares around with your thumbs to get all the scrambled numbers in order. The only problem with using that kind of puzzle as a model for a stained glass window is that there always has to be a blank space into which to slide a window pane. It was no problem to put a clear glass window behind the entire stained glass puzzle to keep the cold air from blowing in, but it just wouldn't look right with a blank square in the middle of all that stained glass. But the artist found a way to use that empty space to his artistic advantage.

When the window was finished, the picture was actually quite simple. It was just a huge Jesus and a small town. The town was nothing special—small, nondescript buildings and houses. Jesus, on the other hand, was glorious. He was tall and slender and handsome, and was standing erect with his feet positioned as if he were walking. His hair was a deep golden brown that by contrast made his blue eyes seem to shoot out of his face. His clothes were the whitest white you have ever seen and his halo was so yellow it looked like God had just polished it with a cloud. During the morning worship service—when it was a clear day and the sun seemed to be shooting all its rays directly at the window—you almost couldn't look at Jesus without squinting because he was so bright and glorious.

Now the window was made of fifteen sliding panes plus that one extra space, so that it was four panes high and four panes wide. And it was designed to be set in one of two positions. When the panes were in the first position, Jesus was standing on the left side of the window walking away from the town. The small town was to the right, behind Jesus, with the empty pane being in the upper right-hand corner. On the stained-glass panes just below the empty space was the picture of a pole that ran up to the empty space. Painted on the clear glass up in the corner, so that it looked like it was part of the stained glass and connected to that pole, was a road sign with the town name on it: *Jerusalem.* So, you see, in this position, the window portrayed Jesus having just been raised from the dead in all his glory, departing from Jerusalem so that he could meet his disciples back in Galilee.

Now when the panes were slid around one at a time so that finally they got into the second position, Jesus was over on the right and town was over on the left. This way it looked like Jesus was *approaching* the town. And this time the empty space was in the upper left-hand corner, and it also had a road sign painted on the clear glass behind it. This sign, however, read, *Tinyville.* In the first position the window showed the resurrected Jesus leaving Jerusalem and headed for Galilee; in the second position it portrayed the glorified Jesus returning to Tinyville. That new window was truly something else to behold. Surely it would make Jesus want to come to Tinyville before he went anywhere else.

The Tinyville World Scope, of course, wanted some pictures of the window for the front page of the paper. That meant they needed Mr. Romano. He was the only person around who could make a black and white photograph do justice to that colorful window.

When the editor tried to hire him, Mr. Romano laughed and said he would do it for free. The irony of the town having to hire an atheist they all disliked to take a picture of the mythical Jesus they adored was payment enough for him. He did require, however, that he be left alone to do his work. He wouldn't have busybody church people hovering over him like a bunch of clumsy angels while he was trying to create art with his camera.

So as a favor to the editor, the trustees at Resurrection Church reluctantly agreed to let Mr. Romano have his way, and they shut him up in the sanctuary to do his work one Friday around nine o'clock in the morning so that he could catch the best light. But they stayed right outside the door in the narthex the whole time. It was about six hours before Mr. Romano finally opened the doors and headed out. The trustees bombarded him with questions:

"Well, did you get a good shot?"

"Was the light OK?"

"How are the pictures going to look?"

"What took you so long?"

But Mr. Romano didn't answer any of their inquiries. He just walked straight out of the church and muttered to himself, "He really is God's Son. Go figure. He really is."

The trustees were all amazed. At first they just stood there staring at the open door. Then they stared at each other. Finally,

Mr. Peterson spoke up: "We did it! We presented Christ's resurrection and return with such power that even God's own enemy has seen the light. If that doesn't get Christ to Tinyville, I don't know what will!"

Everybody was terribly anxious to see how the stained-glass window looked through the camera's eye. So when Mr. Romano's photographs arrived in the mail at the newspaper office, the editor invited the Resurrection trustees to a party at his house to be there when he opened the envelope and saw them for the first time.

But what a shock they got. Not a single photo showed the window as it was supposed to be. There wasn't one shot of Christ's resurrection in Jerusalem, nor one of his return to Tinyville. Instead, Mr. Romano had taken pictures of the window when the panes were all out of order, when Christ was scrambled and the town was in pieces. Jesus and the town were all mixed together. And in each photograph, the empty space was in a different place, never in one of the top two corners where it was supposed to be. And if that wasn't enough, the photographs weren't even in focus; the stained glass was all blurry.

They spread all of the photos out on the coffee table and looked at them in disgust. "Not a good one in the bunch," some man said. I heard him say it because it was right at that point that Mark, the editor's son, and I came running into the living room. We had been out swimming in the pond, and as soon as we came in the editor shouted at Mark, "Young man what are you doing in here all but naked while I'm entertaining guests. At least, wrap your towel around yourself." It was at that point that Mark noticed the photographs and said, "These are great pictures," and he picked up one to look at more closely.

"Great?" choked my Daddy, who was one of the trustees. "Those are the worst pictures I've ever seen. Jesus is all messed up, and everything is all out of focus."

"They're not out of focus," Mark replied. And he backed up his claim by pointing to the photograph he was holding. All of the trustees leaned over to look at the photograph more closely a second time, and sure enough, part of it was in focus.

Through the empty pane, at a distance, in clear focus, you could see Bart. Bart always sat on the corner of Main and Oak begging for change. He was the only blind man in Tinyville.

The trustees and the newspaper editor started rechecking all of the photos and, sure enough, in every one of them the focus was on what could be seen at a distance through the empty pane, beyond the scrambled Jesus and broken-apart town. What the photograph revealed depended on where the empty space was. In one you could see the three shanties set up behind the general store. In another you could see the dirty children coming out of the machine factory at the end of their long workday. In the third one you could see two policemen arresting a prostitute. In a different photo you could see a small wooden house that needed painting and roofing work done on it. In front of the house was a notice of an upcoming foreclosure auction. Another photograph through the empty pane showed a mother with four children gathered at a graveside with a priest. In the last picture, the empty pane revealed a burned cross standing beside a tree that had a noose hanging from a lower limb.

After that second look at the photos, everyone quit talking about the return of Jesus. And every Sunday the trustees scrambled the window into a different position. Being just a kid, I didn't really understand what had happened, so I finally asked Daddy why we didn't worry about Jesus coming back anymore. After a short pause Daddy said, "Because he's been here all along. We just didn't recognize him."

CHAPTER 3

Resurrection in the Gospel
of Matthew: An Easter Foundation

Most preachers learned about the Synoptic Problem in our introductory biblical classes in seminary. We all know that (most likely) Matthew and Luke used Mark as one of their major sources in the writing of their own gospel narratives. The problem is that we have all domesticated this knowledge in our interpretation of Matthew and Luke in the pulpit.

We tend to think of the writing of the synoptic gospels as a straightforward evolutionary process in which the expansion of one gospel into the next was a natural progression. Often, when the literary relationship of Matthew and Luke to Mark is described in summary fashion, it is said that the two later gospel writers used Mark as their primary source, including most of its content and basically following its outline. To Mark, however, they added a great deal of sayings material, for while Mark emphasized Jesus' role as a teacher, he did not report much of Jesus' actual teaching.

But this sort of summary presents a naïve view of the original situation. While Matthew's and Luke's use of Mark as one of their major sources does indeed demonstrate a high appreciation of Mark's religioliterary achievement, the very act of rewriting the story of the Christ Event simultaneously exhibits a strong dissatisfaction with Mark and a critique of Mark's message and theology. The two later gospel writers didn't simply append Mark's gospel. They *changed* it. They took issue with it. And they argued against it.

If preachers are to proclaim Matthew's or Luke's understanding of the Christ Event effectively, they must grapple with the question of why the two later evangelists felt compelled to write a gospel in the first place. Why was Mark's gospel not good enough for Matthew's community? for Luke's community? In this chapter and the next, we will examine Matthew and Luke to see how they offer a powerful critique of Mark's story and especially of Mark's interpretation of the resurrection. In their versions of the Easter story, there is no empty tomb without a risen Jesus. No failed message. No silent, fearful women. No unredeemed disciples. No parable. So what is there?

We turn first to Matthew, who foreshadows Jesus' resurrection at the crucifixion by describing the raising of the saints (27:51–53); places guards at the tomb to demonstrate that Jesus' body wasn't simply stolen (27:62–66; 28:11–15); tells of Jesus' appearing first to the women who came to see the tomb (28:9–10); and ends with the risen Jesus' appearing to the Eleven on a mountain in Galilee and uttering the great commission:

> And Jesus came and said to them, "All authority in heaven and on earth has been given to me. Go therefore and make disciples of all nations, baptizing them in the name of the Father and of the Son and of the Holy Spirit, and teaching them to obey everything that I have commanded you. And remember, I am with you always, to the end of the age." (28:18–20, NRSV)

Matthew as Critic

Most scholars estimate that Matthew was probably written a decade or so after Mark. What might we hypothesize led Matthew to see, in this short amount of time, a need for a new narrative interpretation of the Christ Event?

Mark was written around the year 70 C.E., the point at which the Jewish revolt was quelled by the Romans. Jerusalem was sacked and the temple was destroyed, never to be rebuilt. Because Christianity was still a mixture of Jews and Gentiles and because some Christians had hoped that the revolt signaled the parousia, the defeat represented a crisis of faith for many Christians as well as for Jews. Mark was most likely written, at least in part, in response to this crisis—in order to provide a route through the crisis. A theology primarily rooted in the glory of the resurrection was doomed to collapse when the risen Christ did not return and God did not give victory to the rebels. Thus Mark, in the form of a parable, replaces the risen Christ as the central understanding of Jesus with the narrative portrait of the crucified Son of God.

By the time Matthew wrote his gospel this crisis had well passed. There were certainly lingering effects of the defeat and destruction of Jerusalem and the temple for Christianity, but the immediacy of the failure of the parousia as part of the hopes surrounding the Jewish Revolt had passed.

Church and Synagogue

Following the defeat of the Jewish Revolt, Judaism underwent a major transformation, with Pharisaic Judaism centered in the study of rabbinic teachings in the context of the synagogue replacing the now-defunct temple cult. As Judaism was being transformed in the later decades of the first century, so did the church's relationship with Judaism change. The church was growing ever more Gentile. The difference in Jewish and Christian practices widened, and Christians and Jews were interpreting Hebrew Scriptures in more and more contradictory fashions. By Matthew's time the conflict between the changing synagogue and the changing church was in full force, and the task of Christianity's self-definition was a tense one.

Matthew's community was not completely without resources in this process. They could turn to Mark's gospel and find a few helpful elements to guide them in this struggle for self-definition. For example,

- Mark opens with a scripture quotation (1:2–3), thus intimating that the entire story of the Christ Event is a fulfillment of scripture. This is especially evident in the passion narrative, where much of the story is shaped to echo Psalm 22.

- Mark portrays Jesus as being in conflict with Jewish authorities throughout his ministry and always besting them. Some of these conflicts deal with ritual and Sabbath observance and thus redefine a Christian ethos over against a Jewish one (2:1–28; 3:1–6, 22–27; 7:1–23; 8:11–21, 10:2–9; 11:27–12:40).

- Mark frames Jesus' cursing of the temple (11:15–18) with the cursing (11:12–14) and withering (11:19–21) of the fig tree. The literary technique may be read as implying that as Jesus' cursing of the fig tree caused the tree to wither, so his cursing of the temple caused it to be destroyed. This theological claim justifies the church's move away from Judaism.

But these sorts of texts do not provide enough resources to define and defend the church over against its parent Judaism once the conflict has risen to a higher level, once new Jewish and Christian institutional structures have begun to evolve.

Therefore, Matthew must deem Mark inadequate for the needs of the day and choose to write a gospel that equips his community for the conflict. The equipping takes place in several ways. First, Matthew's narrative emphasizes an interpretation of the Christ Event as the fulfillment of scripture. Like Mark, there are places where Matthew makes the assertion that Jesus fulfills scripture in a somewhat subtle manner. For example, while Matthew never explicitly says so, his characterization of Jesus is modeled on the scriptural figure Moses. It is beyond our scope to detail all the places where Matthew does this, but for our purposes it is important to notice that, like Moses, Jesus' most important teachings come from the mountaintop (e.g., the Sermon on the Mount [chaps. 5–7] and the great commission [28:16–20]). But unlike Mark, Matthew also explicitly asserts, over and over again, that something Jesus did or said, something that happened to Jesus, or something related to the Christ Event was done to fulfill scripture (1:22–23; 2:5–6, 15, 17–18, 23; 3:3; 4:14–16; 12:17–21; 13:35; 27:9–10; see also 26:54, 56).

Second, in addition to Matthew's reinterpreting scripture so that it applies to Jesus, the evangelist presents Jesus himself as interpreting scripture in a fashion that would challenge other contemporary interpretations, that is, interpretations offered by Pharisaic Judaism. The key passage occurs in 5:17–48, where Jesus claims that his teaching fulfills the law and offers six antitheses ("You have heard...but I say to you...") that demonstrate Jesus' hermeneutical method of fulfilling the law. Jesus fulfills the *torah* not by meeting its demands, but by completing them, by drawing out the torah's radical, hidden implications. The command not to murder is intensified to include a prohibition against anger. The command not to commit adultery includes a prohibition against lust. The command not to swear falsely really means that one should be honest enough that she or he need not be called upon to swear at all. The list goes on, but the six antitheses are clearly not meant to be exhaustive. They are examples of the hermeneutic Matthew's community should use when interpreting *torah*. And, indeed, Matthew's offering of this exemplary hermeneutic legitimizes reading Matthew's own narrative in a similar fashion. As Matthew demonstrated the "completion" of *torah* for his community, so should modern readers follow his hermeneutic of completion for our communities. In other words, interpreters are not allowed the luxury of reading Matthew at a surface level. To be true to the examples provided by the gospel writer himself in the Sermon on the Mount, we must dig into Matthew's text to discover the deeper, hidden implications that accord with a modern worldview. This is especially true when we speak of interpreting Matthew's resurrection narrative.

A third way Matthew's narrative equips the church to deal with its conflict with the synagogue is by presenting the Jewish leaders and populace as playing a stronger role in Jesus' execution than Mark had asserted. This happens in several ways:

- Just prior to the passion narrative, Matthew expands verses in Mark (12:38–40) in which Jesus denounces the scribes into a thirty-six–verse-long speech (Mt. 23:1–36) in which Jesus accuses the scribes and Pharisees of hypocrisy in great detail. Following on the heels of conflict between Jesus and these Jewish authorities throughout the narrative, this verbal attack sets up the reader to view the Jewish authorities in an extremely negative light in the passion narrative.

- And they are so presented in the passion narrative. In the trial before the Sanhedrin, Mark writes that testimony against Jesus was sought (14:55), but Matthew alters this to say that *false* testimony was sought (26:59), implying a much more vicious intent. In the same scene, when asked whether he is the Christ, Jesus is presented as answering differently in the two gospels. Mark has him say point blank, "I am" (14:62), but Matthew keeps Jesus' answer ambiguous ("*You* have said so," 26:64), so that the chief priests have no real evidence on which to take Jesus to Pilate.

- In the trial scene before Pilate (27:11–26), Matthew goes to great lengths to present the Roman governor as resisting the Jewish desire to have Jesus executed, thus placing even more emphasis on the Jewish conflict. When Jesus has given no response to his accusers, Pilate wonders *greatly*. Knowing that the Jewish leaders are acting out of envy, Pilate offers to release Jesus or a notorious prisoner, Barabbas, but the Jewish leaders choose Barabbas. Pilate's wife has a dream that Jesus is a righteous man and sends word for the governor to have nothing to do with him. Finally, Pilate washes his hands and claims to be innocent of Jesus' blood, and Matthew has "all the people" respond, "His blood be upon us and our children."

Modern preachers must be careful neither to interpret these elements as signs of Matthew's being anti-Jewish nor to use Matthew to support modern anti-Semitism. Matthew was struggling to offer the church a way to continue growing independent of the synagogue even while valuing its Jewish foundation. Thus, an appreciation of scripture is enhanced, while the contrast between late-first-century Christianity and Judaism is simultaneously sharpened.

A final way that Matthew equips the church in its task of self-definition over against the synagogue is to offer a schematized understanding of the inclusion of Gentiles in the church. Although we did not examine the motif of Gentile inclusion in Mark in our last chapter, Mark is concerned with this issue. Without going into detail, it is safe to say that Matthew again finds Mark much too subtle on this point. So Matthew presents Jesus himself as specifically setting up a chronological progression for the church to follow. When he commissions the Twelve and sends them out with authority to exorcise demons, heal the sick, and preach the good news, he orders them to go nowhere among the Gentiles/nations (Gk. *ethnoi*) or the Samaritans but only to the lost sheep of the house of Israel (10:5). These instructions are not found in Mark's version of the commission (6:7–11) On the other hand, Matthew deletes Mark's reference to the return of the Twelve (Mk. 6:30). Thus, Matthew describes the mission within the span of his ministry as being to the Jews, but the mission to the Jews is never closed. It remains open even at the end of the gospel (28:19), where Jesus' great commission for the Eleven specifies that they are to make disciples of all nations/Gentiles (Gk. *ethnoi*). Thus, the synagogue may argue that the pre-passion mission of Jesus and his followers was within the confines of Judaism, but Matthew equips his readers to argue that Jesus himself instructed the postresurrection church to move beyond the mission of the precrucifixion movement, that Jesus himself moved the church to include both Jews and Gentiles.

The Church

The other basis for Matthew's judgment that Mark was inadequate to continue meeting the needs of his community may have been related to the passing of the immediate crisis that Mark addressed in a different way. The fall of Jerusalem was ten to twenty years in the past. The church must begin to look to the future. It needed a document that would serve as a foundation for its beliefs, mission, ethics, and communal life. A gospel that serves as an imaginative and powerful critique of a resurrection theology cannot serve well as a primary, foundational document for generations of a community. Therefore, Matthew uses material from Mark's gospel, but radically alters the orientation of that material so that a new story of the Christ Event can serve as a foundation. This new orientation is manifested in several ways.

First, Matthew offers a more balanced view of the disciples than is found in Mark's gospel. The parabolic, ironic bumbling of the disciples in Mark is not conducive to a foundational document, when they are clearly the ones responsible for passing the faith down to Matthew's generation. While the Twelve certainly still exhibit misunderstanding at times, they also exhibit faithfulness and great insight. For example, we remember that in Mark, Jesus immediately silences Peter when Peter claims Jesus is the Messiah and not Son of God (8:30). But in Matthew 16:16–19, Peter professes Jesus to be "the Messiah, the Son of the living God," and Jesus responds:

> Blessed are you, Simon son of Jonah! For flesh and blood has not revealed this to you, but my Father in heaven. And I tell you, you are Peter, and on this rock I will build my church, and the gates of Hades will not prevail against it. I will give you the keys of the kingdom of heaven, and whatever you bind on earth will be bound in heaven, and whatever you loose on earth will be loosed in heaven. (NRSV)

So Peter's correct answer leads to his appointment as the foundation of the church (Gk. *ecclesia*) and to his reception of authority in matters calling for judgment, even though in Jesus' next breath he is forced to rebuke Peter (16:22–23). This pattern of redeeming the image of the disciples recurs throughout the first gospel.

As Jesus is presented as granting Peter the authority to bind and loose in chapter 16, later Matthew presents Jesus as giving this same authority to the whole church (18:18). Indeed, the second way Matthew alters Mark so that it may serve as a foundational document is to present Jesus as directly dictating church rule for Matthew's community. We noticed in Jesus' response to Peter, Matthew has Jesus anachronistically use the term "church" (Gk. *ecclesia*, 16:18). This happens twice more in 18:17. Because there was no "church" in Jesus' day, clearly the narrative setting of the discourse in chapter 18—a dialogue between Jesus and his disciples—is a transparent veil for

Matthew's using the narrative to establish, confirm, or reform behavior in his own community in his own day. For example, central to the discourse is Jesus' dictation of the reconciliation procedure to be followed in the church when one person in the community sins against another (18:15–20). This would become an issue only as the community of faith became more stable and institutionalized.

The third way Matthew changes Mark to write a foundational instead of reactionary narrative is by greatly expanding the teachings of Jesus that are narrated. Mark is primarily concerned with the proper understanding of Jesus' identity and his readers' response to that identity. While Matthew is certainly concerned with christology, he wants to demonstrate the legacy of both Jesus' identity and preaching for the contemporary (i.e., 80s) church. As is well known, Matthew spreads Jesus' teachings throughout his narrative but concentrates a great deal of his sayings into five discourses. We have already mentioned some of them, but by briefly looking at the five together we can see how Matthew organizes this material to serve the needs of an ongoing community of faith. The discourses are somewhat loosely organized around topics, and each ends with a transitional stylized formula on the order of "When Jesus had finished saying these things..." The fifth discourse ends with the phrase "When Jesus had finished saying *all* these things..." and then moves to the plot to kill Jesus. Therefore, the five discourses demonstrate the core of Jesus' teaching, which in the narrative world plays a role in his being perceived as a threat by the Jewish authorities, and which in Matthew's world served as the core of Jesus' teaching still needed for his community:

- *5:1–7:29, Ethical Discourse.* As the first public speech of Jesus in Matthew, the Sermon on the Mount is especially powerful and deserves the attention it has always received. In the narrative, the speech is addressed to the disciples with the crowd overhearing, but clearly it is Matthew addressing his community as they struggle to shape their ethos over against the synagogue. The discourse focuses on the hermeneutics for understanding the legal and ethical imperatives of Hebrew Scripture, the appropriate nature of religious practice, and an array of other ethical and pious concerns.

- *10:1–11:1, Missionary Discourse.* Again, this discourse is narrated as Jesus' addressing the Twelve as he sends them out with his authority to do the same work he has done (exorcisms, healing, preaching the dominion of God). But it is clearly meant to guide and encourage Matthew's church as they struggle to spread the gospel in difficult times. The discourse describes the proper behavior and expectations of those sent out from the church. Especially significant for Matthew's community is how to do the missionary work in the face of late-first-century persecution.

- *13:1–53, Parabolic Discourse.* Matthew has taken much of the material of this discourse over from Mark. But the manner in which he edits the material is significant. When Mark has Jesus describe why he preaches in parables, Jesus says that he preaches this way to those outside "in order that [Gk. *hina*] 'they may look, but not perceive…'" (4:12). Matthew makes a subtle but extremely significant alteration. Jesus says, "The reason I speak to them [simply distinguishing the crowds ("them") from the disciples instead of insiders and outsiders] in parables is that [Gk. *dia touto*,"because"] 'seeing they do not perceive…'" (13:13). Thus, instead of serving as a narrative technique in which the outsiders are kept outside the dominion of God in their misunderstanding, in Matthew the parables are tools by which those who do not understand are offered the opportunity to come to understanding. In a foundational narrative, parables need to serve the purpose of illumination, not discrimination.

- *18:1–19:1, Community Discourse.* We have already discussed how, in this discourse, Matthew prescribes some communal behavior patterns in terms of dealing with conflict within the community. More than any of the other discourses, this one shows Matthew's concern with offering the church resources to guide its continued, institutionalized existence.

- *24:1–26:1, Eschatological Discourse.* Matthew's concern for the ongoing life of the community does not eliminate hope for the parousia. As with other discourses, a major portion of this discourse comes from Mark, but again Matthew alters it to serve the needs of a foundational narrative. For example, Matthew removes much of Mark's language concerning persecution and places it in his missionary discourse. Because Matthew's community has been enduring persecution since Mark's time, it should not be mistaken as a sign of the end time. On the other hand, Matthew increases the content concerning false messiahs and prophets to lessen the amount of uninformed speculation about the parousia that would arise as the church became increasingly impatient, but adds sayings that emphasize the need to keep waiting and watching.

A fourth way that Matthew alters Mark to reduce the parabolic character of the narrative and replace it with foundational elements, and the most important way for our purposes, is to extend the beginning of the narrative back from Jesus' baptism to his birth and to complete the story of the resurrection. This addition of the beginning and the completion of the ending of the story of the Christ Event should not be interpreted as two independent moves on the part of Matthew. The material prior to the Ethical Discourse and following the Eschatological Discourse work together to frame the whole narrative. This framing is achieved by numerous parallels between the two sections. Some of the parallels cited below are stronger than others, but the cumulative effect is undeniable. We list them in order of the appearance of the elements in the final section, since our focus is on the ending of the gospel.

- Both sections are set in both Jerusalem and Galilee. Although Jesus is born in Bethlehem (2:1), the story of Herod and the magi begins in Jerusalem (2:2). Upon returning from Egypt, Joseph takes the family to Nazareth in Galilee (2:22–23), and the section closes with the beginning of Jesus' ministry in Galilee (4:12–25). Most of the material in the closing section of the narrative (Last

Supper, arrest, trials, execution, empty tomb) is set in Jerusalem (26:1–28:15), but the section closes with an appearance of the risen Jesus in Galilee (28:16–20).

- In both sections, Jewish leaders gather as part of the persecution of Jesus (2:4; 26:3, 57).

- In the opening section, the magi bring myrrh to honor Jesus (2:11), and in the final section Jesus is anointed with costly ointment (26:6–13).

- In the temptation scene, the devil invites Jesus to turn stones into bread (4:3), claims angels will bear him up if he jumps from the pinnacle of the temple (4:5–6), and on a mountaintop offers Jesus all the kingdoms of the world if he will worship Satan (4:8–9). In the last section of the gospel, bread plays a role in the Last Supper (26:26); Jesus appeals to God for angels while praying in the garden (26:53), and while on the cross he is mocked: "Let God deliver him now" (27:43); the narrative closes with the disciples' worshiping Jesus on a mountain (28:16–17).

- Forgiveness of sins is a theme that frames Matthew. The angel tells Joseph in a dream that Jesus will save his people from their sins (1:21), and the people confess their sins as they are baptized by John (3:6). During the last supper with his disciples, Jesus refers to the wine as "my blood...which is poured out for many for the forgiveness of sins" (26:28). Compare also 27:42, where the crucified Jesus is mocked with the words "He saved others; he cannot save himself."

- The nearness of the kingdom of heaven is emphasized in both sections. In the opening section, both John the Baptist and Jesus proclaim, "Repent, for the kingdom of heaven has come near" (3:2; 4:17). In the final section, at the end of the Last Supper, Jesus says, "I will never again drink of this fruit of the vine until that day when I drink it new in my Father's kingdom" (26:29).

- In the opening section, the chief priests and scribes cite Micah 5:2 as evidence that the Messiah would be born in Bethlehem. Part of the citation reads, "'from you shall come a ruler who is to shepherd my people Israel'" (2:6).

On the Mount of Olives after the Last Supper, Jesus prophesies that the disciples will desert him and cites Zechariah 13:7 as evidence: "'I will strike the shepherd, and the sheep of the flock will be scattered'" (26:31).

- In the first section, John the Baptist is arrested (4:12), and Jesus is arrested in the final section (26:47–56).

- In the opening section, the ruler in Jerusalem (King Herod) attempts to kill Jesus because he is called king of the Jews (2:1–3, 13, 16–18). In the final section, the ruler in Jerusalem (Governor Pilate) kills Jesus, who is accused of claiming to be and who is mocked as being king of the Jews (27:11, 17, 22, 27–31, 37, 42).

- Dreams (Gk. *onar*) are mentioned only in these two sections. Joseph and the magi are warned of Herod's plot in dreams (2:12, 13, 19); Pilate's wife warns the governor to have nothing to do with Jesus because of her dreams (27:19).

- At Jesus' baptism the voice declares him to be God's Son (3:17) after the angel has declared that he is conceived by the Holy Spirit (1:18, 20; compare also 2:15; 4:3, 6). At Jesus' death, the centurion claims Jesus is truly God's Son (27:54) after the crowd mocks him as claiming he is God's Son (27:40, 43; see also 26:63).

- John the Baptist is modeled on Elijah in 3:1–4 (see also 11:14). And at the cross bystanders think Jesus is calling out to Elijah (27:46–47).

- There is a strong apologetic motif in both sections to counter scandals concerning rumors about Jesus' birth and death. In the first section, the scandal involves the tradition of Jesus' birth to a virgin. The scandal in Matthew's day is brought into the narrative by having Joseph wish to divorce Mary, assuming that she has been unfaithful (1:19). An angel makes it clear to Joseph that the child has been conceived by the Holy Spirit instead of by an illicit lover (1:20). But the narrator also includes women in the opening genealogy to demonstrate that Israel's salvation history has been moved along numerous times by God's use of scandalous women: Tamar, who disguised herself as a prostitute to have a child by her father-in-law, who had denied her the right of levirate marriage (1:3); Rahab, the prostitute who saved the lives of the Israelite spies at Jericho (1:5); Ruth, the Moabite grandmother of David (1:5); the wife of Uriah (Bathsheba), whom David stole from a soldier but who eventually gave birth to Solomon (1:6); and finally Mary (1:16). The scandal addressed at the end of the gospel involves rumors that Jesus was not resurrected, but that instead his body was stolen from the tomb by his disciples (27:64). To counter this accusation, Matthew narrates a story in which guards, placed at the tomb to prevent such a robbery, witness the resurrection and are bribed to tell no one what they saw (27:62–66; 28:11–15).

- While angels are mentioned by Jesus in the middle sections of the narrative (13:39, 41, 49; 16:27; 18:10; 22:30; 24:31, 36; 25:31, 41; 26:53), they appear as characters acting in the story only in the first (1:20, 24; 2:13, 19; 4:11) and final (28:2, 5) sections.

- As Jesus begins his ministry in Galilee (4:12), so does the risen Jesus appear to the disciples in Galilee (28:7, 16–19).

- As the magi pay homage to Jesus in the beginning (2:2, 11), the disciples worship Jesus at the end of the narrative (28:17).

- Both sections emphasize the inclusion of Gentiles in Matthew's understanding of Christianity. In the first, the magi from the East come to pay homage to Jesus (2:1–12); John the Baptist warns that God can raise up new children of Abraham (3:9); and the location of Jesus' ministry is referred to as Galilee of the Gentiles (4:15). In the last section, Jesus' final instructions focus on making disciples of all nations (28:19).

- Baptism plays a role in both sections. In the first chapters, John baptizes crowds (3:6) and Jesus (3:13–16) and speaks of Jesus' baptizing with fire and the Holy Spirit (3:11–12). Jesus' final commission is to send disciples out to baptize all nations in the name of the Father, Son, and Holy Spirit (28:19).

- In the first section the disciples are called to follow Jesus (4:18–22), and in the final section they are commissioned to go out to all nations (28:16–20).

- Prior to his birth, Jesus is called Emmanuel, "God with us" (1:23). At the end of the narrative, Jesus promises to be with the disciples to the end of the age (28:20).

These parallels make it clear that as Matthew edited and appended Mark to create a foundational narrative for his community, he closely connected the expanded ending to the new beginning. The two sections frame the entire narrative of Jesus' ministry, teaching, and travels. And thus, we are justified in reading the ending of Matthew's gospel in light of the beginning, in asserting that from a Matthean perspective, Christmas and Easter (incarnation and resurrection) are integrally related.

The introductory section can be interpreted as focusing on the meaning of Jesus' incarnational identity as "God with us." As Emmanuel, Jesus' preaching and healing were signs of God's presence in Jesus' ministry. The challenge for the late-first-century church was to claim that Jesus was *still* a sign of God's presence even after the crucifixion. The resurrection narrative builds toward Jesus' final words, "And remember, I am with you always, to the end of the age" (28:20), and is thus meant to address the theological challenge of interpreting God's continuing presence in Christ for Matthew's community.

Resurrection

With the exception of the resurrection narrative, Matthew follows Mark fairly closely in the post–Eschatological Discourse section of his story of the Christ Event. The stories are all there:

- The Anointing: 26:6–13
- Judas's Betrayal: 26:14–16
- The Last Supper: 26:17–35
- Prayer and Arrest in Gethsemane: 26:36–56
- The Trials, Denial, and Mocking: 26:57–27:31a
- The Crucifixion: 27:31b–56
- The Burial: 27:57–61

Matthew makes no major narrative additions to or omissions of the Markan material. Nevertheless, by breaking up Mark's earlier narrative with the discourses, diminishing the misunderstanding of the disciples, and adding the Jewish polemic to the narrative, Matthew has all but removed the flavor of an ironic hidden coronation ceremony. No longer do all roads lead to Golgotha. Indeed, all roads lead back to a mountain in Galilee, but you can't get there without going through Golgotha.

The Resurrection Foreshadowed

In fact, even at the cross Matthew makes sure his readers know that resurrection is to follow. Mark narrates the ripping of the temple curtain that accompanies Jesus' death as a sign that the crucifixion has eschatological implications (15:38). Matthew adds to this the following notice:

> The earth shook, and the rocks were split. The tombs also were opened, and many bodies of the saints who had fallen asleep were raised. After his resurrection they came out of the tombs and entered into the holy city and appeared to many. (27:51b–53)

This addition clearly foreshadows that Jesus will be raised from the dead later in Matthew's narrative and thus leaves the readers no room for despair at the cross. Not only is Jesus' resurrection referred to directly, but an earthquake parallels the earthquake that occurs when the angel rolls the stone away from Jesus' tomb in 28:2.

Nevertheless, there is significance to this notice beyond the foreshadowing. The significance revolves around the ambiguous identity of "the *saints* who had fallen asleep," the holy ones who are raised from the dead, and the ambiguous temporal reference concerning their resurrection. This is the only appearance of "saints" (Gk. *hagion*) in the first gospel. Many scholars interpret Matthew's use of the word as referring to the righteous of Israel who died in Jerusalem in the past (e.g., the prophets referred to in 23:37; see also 23:29–36). But one might also assert that it is proper to interpret *hagion* to mean Christian believers as it does in many other New Testament texts, especially the Pauline writings (see Acts 9:13, 32; Rom. 1:7; 8:27; 12:13; 15:25; 1 Cor. 1:2; 6:1; 2 Cor. 1:1; Eph. 2:19; 3:8; Phil. 4:22; Col. 1:4, 26; 1 Tim. 5:10; Heb. 6:10). While we must be careful when interpreting Matthean vocabulary on the basis of writers other than Matthew, this interpretation would fit with Matthew's tendency to place the concerns of his present-day community into the narrative of the Christ Event, as did his anachronistic use of *ecclesia* earlier in the gospel. This second understanding of *hagion* seems implied by the fact that Matthew asserts that the saints who are raised in coincidence with Jesus' crucifixion do not appear until *after* Jesus' resurrection. Where are we to imagine these raised saints hide out for two days while Jesus was buried? Matthew's logic may be of a theological instead of historical or narrative sense at this point. Therefore, although the addition to Mark's death scene is a clumsy piece of the narrative, its significance should not be missed: Matthew interprets Jesus' death and resurrection as having implications for more than just Jesus. Resurrection is a theological category to be applied to both Jesus and Jesus' followers. In other words, the story of the Christ Event translates into the story of the Christian Event. Instead of simply revealing Jesus' identity, the story of Jesus' passion and resurrection affects Christian meaning, living, and expectations. As Jesus experienced resurrection, so too will Christian believers experience resurrection because of Jesus' death and resurrection.

The Resurrection Scandal

After the crucifixion scene, Matthew, following Mark, tells us that Jesus is buried by Joseph of Arimathea (27:57–61). Matthew, however, removes any ambiguity in the characterization of Joseph. Instead of referring to Joseph as a respected member of the Sanhedrin (who had thus had a hand in Jesus' execution) who was waiting for the dominion of God (Mk. 15:43), Matthew simply claims he was a disciple of Jesus (27:57). This redeeming of Joseph also redeems Jesus' burial. Readers do not get the sense that Jesus' body is quickly shoved in the tomb in a dishonorable manner. Indeed, when the women come to the tomb on the first day of the week, they do not come to anoint Jesus' neglected corpse but come simply as mourners visiting the grave of a loved one (28:1). Removal of this scandal allows Matthew to focus on another issue, another scandal.

This other scandal is unique to Matthew's gospel. It is the story of the guards placed at the tomb (27:62–66; 28:11–15). Scholars have long noted that this story clearly represents an apologetic attempt to counter accusations made by non-Christians during Matthew's own time (see the explicit reference to Matthew's time in 28:15) that Jesus was not raised from the dead, but that instead the disciples removed his body from the tomb and claimed God had raised him. Matthew disarms such an accusation by turning the tables and claiming deceit on the part of the accusers. He presents the assertion that Jesus' body was stolen as a fabrication created by the very Jewish authorities with whom his church is in conflict. According to Matthew, the Jewish leaders request that Pilate place soldiers at the tomb to keep Jesus' body from being stolen because Jesus' claim that he would be raised (16:21; 17:23; 20:19; 26:32) is well known. This actually places nonfollowers at the grave to witness that it is empty when the angel descends and the earthquake rolls the stone away (28:1–4). But they are kept silent about their experience by a bribe offered by the Jewish leaders (28:11–15). Thus, Matthew replaces the silence of the women he found distasteful in Mark's narrative (16:8) with the silence of Jesus' opponents.

The readers are to conclude that not only have the Jewish leaders played a role in the death of Jesus, they are also, to some degree, responsible for keeping the news of his resurrection from being believed. But there is another piece of this scandal to be noticed. Matthew follows Mark in having the centurion at the cross claim Jesus truly is God's Son upon seeing him die (27:54). But no such similar profession follows the epiphany at the empty tomb. In spite of the fact that an earthquake accompanies the resurrection as it had the crucifixion and that the epiphany of the angel is such a powerful experience that the guards shake and become like dead men out of fear, Matthew describes neither the soldiers nor the Jewish leaders as repenting and becoming believers upon witnessing the signs of Jesus' resurrection. Clearly, for Matthew the resurrection is much more than the fact that Jesus' body is no longer in the tomb. Indeed, his body is already gone by the time the stone is rolled away. The stone is rolled away so that the women can see in (28:6), not so that Jesus can get out. Matthew understands the resurrection as more than a bodily resuscitation that leads people to believe Jesus is the Son of God.

For Matthew, the story of the resurrection is an expression of Christian believers' experience of God's presence being revealed even after Jesus' death has taken place. It is a narrative expression of the experience of Matthew's own community that Jesus is somehow present in their own day, some forty years after his crucifixion. It is an interpretation of that presence signifying both promise and calling. While the guards see the angel and the empty tomb, seeing the risen Jesus is reserved for those who have followed Jesus. In other words, like the whole of Matthew's gospel itself, the resurrection is presented not as an evangelistic proof (indeed even some of the disciples doubt when they see the risen Jesus [28:17]), but as an experience reserved for those inside the community of faith. The nature of that experience must be inferred from the two resurrection appearances that Matthew reports, first to the women who came to the tomb (28:9–10) and then to the disciples in Galilee (28:16–20). In other words, following Matthew's own hermeneutic, we must uncover the theological implications lying under the surface of the resurrection story.

The Resurrection Appearances

As we have already noted, the women come to the tomb not to complete the burial ritual as in Mark, but presumably to honor their loved one. Matthew simply says that they "went to see the tomb" (28:1). This means they are not concerned about how to roll the stone away, because they do not intend to do so. But when they arrive at the tomb, there is an earthquake accompanied by the appearance of an angel who does roll the stone away, so that they might know that Jesus is no longer there (28:2). The appearance and the words of the angel (28:3–8) closely parallel those of the young man in Mark's story, whom Matthew also omits from the arrest scene (see 26:47–56).

The women's response, however, is radically different than in Mark's gospel. In Matthew their fear is complemented by great joy, and instead of keeping silent they obediently run to tell Jesus' disciples that he is risen and is going ahead of them to Galilee (28:8). Their joy (Gk. *charas*) is rewarded with greetings (Gk. *chairete*, a standard greeting meaning something like "Good day" but that literally means "rejoice") from the risen Jesus (28:9). And even though Jesus was raised from the dead without the stone's being moved from the entrance of the tomb, the women can "take hold of his feet" and worship him (28:9). Matthew either does not sense or simply does not attempt to resolve the tension between asserting on the one hand that Jesus left the tomb by passing through the physical reality of the stone walls and door and on the other hand that Jesus can be physically touched. The point would seem to be that Jesus' mysterious presence in Matthew's community is so real that it can be described in both manners, and indeed it is so real that it evokes worship not of a God of the past but of a God who is present.

Likewise, when the eleven disciples go to Galilee and meet Jesus on the mountain, they are also described as worshiping Jesus (28:17). Such behavior had not been attributed to the disciples prior to Jesus' death and resurrection. This worshipful response should be seen as parallel to that of the centurion at the cross. As the witness to the crucifixion professes Jesus as God's son (27:54), so the witnesses of the resurrection (i.e., those who experience the resurrected Jesus as God's presence) worship Jesus (28:17). This repetition of the worship motif shows that Matthew's theology of the resurrection is key to his creation of a foundational document. In other words, it is through encountering the risen Jesus Christ that the church *is* the church and is able to fulfill its mission.

The gospel as a whole ends with Jesus' short pronouncement to those who now worship him (28:18–20), implying that the mission of the church grows out of the church's worshipful encounter with the risen Jesus. As already mentioned, this pronouncement takes place on a mountain in Galilee (28:16). Mountains are symbolic spaces for Matthew, and understanding how they are used earlier in the narrative sharpens our understanding of this scene.

- In 4:8 the devil takes Jesus to a mountain and offers him all the kingdoms of the world if he will worship the devil. Jesus refuses and quotes scripture that says, "Worship the Lord your God, and serve only him." Now on this final mountain, the readers see Jesus being worshiped and claiming that all authority in heaven and on earth has been given to him. Through his death and resurrection, Jesus has achieved what Satan offered him. Moreover, Jesus is now worthy of worship, which was denied to the devil because worship is due only to God. Following the resurrection, therefore, Jesus achieves or is revealed as possessing a divine status. (We should be careful not to exaggerate this narrative implication into a full-blown Trinitarian theology, even though Matthew does give testimony to the practice of baptizing in the name "of the Father, and of the Son and of the Holy Spirit" [28:19]).

- In 5:1, Jesus goes up on a mountain (in Galilee) to deliver to his disciples the Ethical Discourse we call the Sermon on the Mount (5:1–8:1). This discourse represents Jesus' first direct speech in the narrative other than the summary of his preaching that Matthew offers in 4:17. Now at the end of the narrative, Jesus returns to a mountain in Galilee to speak his final words. Surely, readers are to presume it is the same mountain to which Jesus returns. And, therefore, the mountain serves as a framing device that leads the readers to seek a connection between his final declaration and his pre-passion teaching. Indeed, in 28:20 Jesus commissions the Eleven to teach everything that he had commanded of them. Earlier in the narrative only Jesus was presented as teaching. The mountain setting makes it clear that the content of their teaching should be both the identity of Jesus himself and the content of Jesus' teaching.

- In 17:1–9 Jesus takes Peter, James, and John up a mountain, where he is transfigured and Elijah and Moses (who are also known for their own mountaintop experiences) appear with him. The voice from heaven echoes the voice at baptism revealing to the three disciples that Jesus is God's "Son, the Beloved." Clearly, the appearance of the risen Jesus on a mountain at the end of the narrative is meant to imply a revelation of Jesus' identity that confirms this epiphany.

As at the transfiguration, where Peter was not allowed to construct tents so that they could remain on the mountain (17:4), Jesus' last words send the Eleven down from the mountain where they have experienced resurrection. His first last word is "Go" (28:19). Jesus does not invite the disciples to stay and worship in joy endlessly. The goal is not to revel in the experience of the resurrected Jesus, but to share the experience. The disciples are to go forth baptizing and teaching; in sum, making disciples of all nations (Gk. *ethnoi*), expanding the mission far beyond its precrucifixion boundaries. The narrative use of the Galilean mountain is not a return to the past, but exactly the opposite. It is the starting point from which the church is to move into its future. While there is to be an appreciation of, even an anchoring in, Jewish scripture, the Christian community is no longer to seek being Jewish. It is to be a community of all nations, of all Gentiles. Matthew presents a new hermeneutic, new teaching, new ritual for a new day. It is the experience of the resurrection of Jesus Christ that confirms this new day, this eschatological day, because the experience of the resurrection is the fulfilling of Jesus' closing promise: "I am with you always, to the end of the age." This experience of the resurrection expressed in the form of a promise concerning the ongoing presence of God is a foundation on which a community can be built and move into the future.

And indeed, it is this experience of the resurrection of Jesus Christ that those of us preaching Matthew's version of the Easter story should attempt to make available to our congregations. Matthew does not simply tell a story about what happened in first-century Jerusalem and Galilee. The gospel offers us an eschatological vision of experiencing divine presence in *our* lives and *our* world. This mysterious experience is foundational for the Christian life and Christian community. In other words, experience of the divine presence of Jesus Christ that evokes nothing short of worship is that which leads to true discipleship and evangelism. It is by empowering congregations to experience the resurrection of Jesus Christ in their own lives that we preachers "make disciples" who are committed to living out the good news of Jesus Christ as portrayed throughout the rest of the first gospel.

Spontaneous Worship (Mt. 28:1–10)

Once I was serving as a faculty sponsor for a student service trip to Nigeria. There had been many disappointing elements to the trip, not the least of which was the fact that our group had been kept rather isolated and had had little chance for authentic, informal interaction with the townspeople and their local culture. One night, after an especially frustrating day, I was trying to sleep on my foam mattress on the concrete floor at about 1:00 a.m. in eighty-degree weather. Lying as still as I could so as not to make myself sweat any more than I already did, I was jolted out of bed by an unexpected, very loud triangle being rung outside my window. It sounded like an old ranch bell used to call the workers in from the field to dinner. It rang for a good thirty seconds or so before the silence settled back in.

I had no clue why the triangle was being rung but was aware that there had been a recent death at the compound across the dirt road from where we were staying. There had been many extended mourning rituals, like cannon fire one morning at 6:15 to mark the end of twelve days of honoring the deceased, so I assumed this was another such ritual.

About ten minutes later, however, I began to hear a voice singing...and then two voices...and then more. The bell had obviously been calling people together, but not just for singing. By 1:30 the drums and cowbells and flutes were in full force accompanying the singing. I couldn't believe it. I had to get up early in the morning and accompany students to the construction site and watch them work...I needed my sleep! But drums pounding, flutes tweeting, metal banging, and voices squalling made sleep out of the question.

My frustration reached a fever pitch, until I finally got up off the floor and went upstairs to sit on the balcony. We had no electricity, so it was pitch dark. I sat and listened to the music and the chanting in Igbo, contemplating how a culture could allow people to be so rude to neighbors so late at night.

The same song went on for nearly thirty minutes nonstop. I was whining inside my head—I won't tell you exactly the words that came to mind so that I can retain my image as a pure, holy man. But the thoughts you'd expect were there. And then I noticed it. I don't know how long it had been going on, but my foot had been tapping to the beat. Even while I was complaining, the rhythm had begun to soak into my bones. I realized that, actually, this was the very Africa I had been frustrated that I had not yet gotten to experience.

So instead of just being surrounded by noise, I began attending to the music. I was amazed at how melodic the frenzy seemed once I allowed it to be. And then, in the midst of this tribal-like expression, I heard something. A single word that I recognized. In the midst of the song was sounded a word common to both Igbo and English—common to both because it came from neither. It was Hebrew. The word was *Hallelujah!* which originally meant "Praise Yahweh!" But since long before Christianity was carried to Ogbunike, Nigeria, Christians have reserved *Hallelujah* for celebrating the victory of the resurrection, and use of the word is prohibited in worship during times of fasting. For instance, songs with *Hallelujah* are avoided during Lent and sought after during Easter. Here was a home, a house-church, that days before had shot a cannon three times to remind the whole community of the death of a loved one and was now singing *Hallelujah* with a driving beat at two o'clock in the morning.

Without consciously doing anything to make it happen, I found myself immersed in a spontaneous worship experience that upon reflection I would describe as experiencing the resurrection itself. The more I thought about it, the more I realized that I have attended many Easter services in my life in which I *really* experienced the resurrection. But hardly any of them involved sermons or hymns or sacraments. Most of them didn't occur in a sanctuary at all. And most of them didn't occur on Easter.

My father is an alcoholic. So many people have lived in homes with an alcoholic family member that I don't need to describe what my experience growing up was like. Throughout all the kinds of things you would expect, I made excuses for Dad and held out hope that he would get better. Until my ordination. At that point in my life, I considered that day to be the most important day of my young adulthood. I was in seminary in Connecticut, and Dad and I had talked about the ordination service back in Alabama numerous times in advance. He was going to be there. But on the day of the ordination he called my in-laws, not me, and told them he was sick and couldn't make it. "Sick," of course, should be translated as drunk. This was not the first time my father had been absent from something important in my life because he was "sick." But I decided it was the last time.

I had reached the point where I could no longer make excuses. I called him and told him that I was not ending our relationship, but instead finally admitting that we hadn't had a real father-son relationship for a long time. I declared myself fatherless. For a while he sent mail, such as birthday cards with checks in them, but I sent them back. The days I received mail from him got farther and farther apart. And then there was silence. There was nothing. There was death.

About a year later my brother called me. Dad had asked him to call because he couldn't call on his own. He had hit rock bottom and was going to put himself into a residential rehabilitation program. Within an hour of the phone call, I was in my car headed south out of Connecticut on a nonstop twenty-something-hour drive to Sylacauga, Alabama.

When I pulled into the driveway at my father's house, the back door opened, and a man I almost didn't recognize stepped out. The illness of alcoholism had taken an extreme toll in a year's time. I got out of the car; Dad grabbed me and I grabbed him and we hugged and wept like we were actors in one of those terribly sappy TV movies where everything wraps up nicely and neatly in the end. If I had seen it on TV, I would have changed the channel. The time we stood there afraid to let go of each other again didn't erase the past, but it did mark an honest-to-goodness new beginning.

Without consciously doing anything to make it happen, I found myself participating in a spontaneous worship experience that I would describe as experiencing the resurrection itself.

I have read the gospel of Matthew enough that I feel as if I know it pretty well. And, of course, I have attended church all my life and have heard the Easter story preached over and over and over again. But it was just recently that something hit me about this story that I had never realized before. I felt stupid when I saw it, because what I noticed is really obvious, but I had just missed it all this time. You know the story. Mary Magdalene and the other Mary go to Jesus' tomb. Suddenly there is an earthquake, and an angel descends from heaven. The angel rolls the stone back from the entrance to the tomb, and those guarding the tomb shake from fear and become like dead men. The angel tells the women to look inside and see that Jesus is not there. The women run from the tomb and bump into Jesus unexpectedly. They grab his feet and worship him there outside the tomb.

Now, what I noticed about this story that I had not noticed before had to do with the stone. I always assumed that the stone was rolled away from the tomb to let Jesus out. But it wasn't. Jesus was already gone. The stone was moved to let the women in, not to let Jesus out. It was rolled away to let the women—not Jesus—experience the resurrection. If that's too subtle for some of us to catch, then Matthew presses the point harder with the contrast between the guards, who are scared to death, and the women, whose joy leads them into an unplanned and unprogrammed worship experience. They look in the tomb, see that it is empty, turn around, grab Jesus, and worship Jesus.

When I realized that Matthew tells the story of the empty tomb to invite *us* to experience resurrection instead of just claiming that something happened to Jesus, I found myself participating in a spontaneous worship experience that I would describe as experiencing the resurrection itself. It made me realize that resurrection rarely happens in church on Easter morning. Indeed, it can't be timed and expected at all. It just happens to us when we least expect, as long as we're open to it. As long as we're willing to look for God where we don't usually expect to find God, as long as we're willing to look into a tomb and find life.

A few years ago, my wife and I visited St. Mark United Methodist Church in Atlanta on a Sunday in late June. The sanctuary was packed, and the service went as you might expect. Following the organ prelude, there were announcements. Then a call to worship and opening prayer, followed by an opening hymn. There was a scripture reading that led first into a children's sermon and then into the adult sermon. There was the offering with an incredible piece of music by the huge choir. Then came prayers and finally a closing hymn and a benediction.

It is difficult for a clergyperson to attend worship that he or she has not planned, or at least it is for me. What I mean is that I sit there and sort of grade everything. "Oh, I would have done that differently." Or, "That's a great idea—I'll use that some time." Once I had begun spending a lot of time planning and leading worship as a part of my weekly job, a Sunday off spent in someone else's church was rarely true worship for me; it was more of a professional assessment experience. This particular Sunday was no different. I watched the way the pastor greeted people and thought I should do more of that before services. I thought the hymns could have been chosen more carefully to fit with the theme of the sermon. I wondered if I agreed with the way the scripture was interpreted and used in the sermon. But I didn't really pray or praise. I wasn't really moved by hearing the good news of Jesus Christ proclaimed. I enjoyed the anthem, but it was more like listening to a performance than being led in sacred meditation. When the service was over, I felt that I had done my Sunday duty, but I didn't really feel that I had worshiped.

After the service, at the front door, we were greeted by the pastor, who was a friend and a colleague. And then we hung around outside at the front of the church with the rest of the congregation. You see, it was Gay Pride Week in Atlanta, and the Gay Pride Parade would be passing in front of the church soon after twelve o'clock. St. Mark had been one of those dying urban churches only a few years before. But when the pastor and congregation opened its doors to the gay community and said that they accepted everyone as a child of God, the congregation came back to life and began to grow and prosper again. Greeting participants in the Gay Pride Parade was one of the ways that St. Mark let homosexuals know that they were welcome to be a part of their community.

The parade began heading toward where we were standing on Peachtree Street when, by coincidence, members of First Baptist Church, which was just across the street, began departing from worship. I watched as a young couple leaving that church literally covered the eyes of their children and rushed them to their cars so that they wouldn't see the parade of "sin." I guess it's no wonder that that church has now abandoned its ministry downtown and moved to one of the wealthier suburbs of Atlanta.

I quit focusing on the Christians across the street running from the parade and began to pay attention to the Christians on my side of the street who were walking out into the parade. It was a hot, humid June day, and those parading were marching down the miles of scorching hot asphalt to proclaim pride in who God made them. And these Christians were performing the simple act of carrying into the crowd cups of ice water to send the marchers on their way with a blessing.

I watched one elderly woman particularly. She was dressed as prim and proper as any older Southern woman ever was. Clearly, she had been a longtime member at St. Mark. She probably had raised a family there back in its heyday in the fifties. She had stayed out of loyalty and habit when the church seemed almost dead. And probably unlike some of her elderly friends, she had remained a part of the church when it opened its doors to those whom many churches reject. And now here she was—in her seventies, maybe eighties—stepping off the curb ever so slowly so as not to fall, walking out into the parade of gays and lesbians and bisexuals and transgender people, where many of the marchers were dressed in odd costumes, some weren't dressed much at all, and some carried snakes around their shoulders. I didn't see this older saint blink an eye at any of them. To anyone who passed close to her, to everyone who passed close to her, she offered the peace of Christ in a paper cup.

Without consciously doing anything to make it happen, I found myself immersed in a spontaneous worship experience that I would describe as experiencing the resurrection itself. I truly worshiped. I truly experienced the presence of the risen Christ.

And who knows, if a hot June afternoon can be transformed into the cool spring dawn of an Easter morning, so perhaps can a cool spring Easter day become a moment of spontaneous worship in which the resurrection is experienced without our consciously doing anything to make it happen. Keep your eyes open. You never know when you might be invited to look into an open tomb and turn around and bump into the risen Christ when you least expect it. If you blink, you might miss it.

CHAPTER 4

Resurrection in the Gospel of Luke: Easter at the Center

We have seen that Matthew's gospel is both an expansion and a critique of Mark's. Luke's narrative theology can also be read as a critique of Mark's usefulness for a new day, but Luke is hardly an expansion of Mark. Whereas Matthew uses approximately 90 percent of Mark's content, Luke only uses about 50 percent. Moreover, his plot structure does not follow Mark nearly as closely as Matthew's. And finally, Luke not only tells the story of the Christ Event, but he adds a second volume that narrates the story of the spread of the good news of Jesus Christ from Jerusalem to Rome.

And indeed, whereas Matthew's strategy for dealing with Mark's incomplete ending was basically to complete it, Luke uses a different ending altogether to the story of the Christ Event. While there is a somewhat similar scene at the empty tomb (24:1–11), Luke keeps the narrative set in Jerusalem and its environs instead of returning to Galilee. The risen Jesus appears first to two disciples (who have not appeared in the narrative prior to this point) on the road to Emmaus and is made known to them in the breaking of bread (24:13–32). He then appears to the Eleven and others in Jerusalem (24:33–49). In this Jerusalem meeting, the risen Jesus instructs the disciples concerning the fulfillment of scripture and says,

Thus it is written, that the Messiah is to suffer and to rise from the dead on the third day, and that repentance and forgiveness of sins is to be proclaimed in his name to all nations, beginning from Jerusalem. You are witnesses of these things. And see, I am sending upon you what my Father promised; so stay here in the city until you have been clothed with power from on high. (NRSV)

Then Luke tells of Jesus' ascension at Bethany and ends the gospel with the disciples' returning to Jerusalem as Jesus had instructed them (24:50–53). Luke's second volume begins by backing up to the time after the resurrection but before the ascension and expands the readers' knowledge of events during that time (Acts 1:1–11). So when we consider Luke's account of the resurrection, we must read it in the full context of Luke–Acts.

Orderly Truth

Unlike the other gospels, Luke–Acts opens with a prologue that explains both the author's methodology in writing and the goals of the narrative:

Since many have undertaken to set down an orderly account of the events that have been fulfilled among us, just as they were handed on to us by those who from the beginning were eyewitnesses and servants of the word, I too decided, after investigating everything carefully from the very first, to write an orderly account for you, most excellent Theophilus, so that you may know the truth concerning the things about which you have been instructed. (Lk. 1:1–4, NRSV)

Luke claims that his narrative is the result of detailed research. He is aware of many other narratives written before his (one of which is clearly Mark). These written narratives are his primary sources, but they themselves used sources: accounts of events handed down by eyewitnesses and servants of the word. So, for his original readers, Luke is offering the lineage of the content of his gospel: He has researched narratives that recorded the memories of eyewitnesses and preachers. (For modern readers, this helps us to know that Luke was actually quite distant from the events about which he was writing; he probably wrote in the late first century.)

The fact that Luke writes his own narrative when there are already so "many" other authors who have written about the Christ Event signals a dissatisfaction with those narratives. The translation of the prologue in the NRSV blurs our look at the primary source of Luke's dissatisfaction by translating two different Greek phrases in the same manner. The NRSV translates Luke's opening clause as "Since many have undertaken to set down *an orderly account...*" A better rendering of the line would be "Since many have undertaken to compile a *narrative...*" (Gk. *epecheiresan anataxasthai diegesin*). The NRSV's rendering of the transitional clause later in the prologue reads, "I too decided, after investigating everything carefully from the very first, to *write an orderly account...*" (Gk. *kathexes... grapsai*). Luke's prologue is one long, carefully crafted sentence. The distinction between compiling a narrative (Gk. *anataxasthai diegesin*) and writing an orderly account (Gk. *kathexes...grapsai)* is significant. Luke seems to be saying that much of his dissatisfaction with his sources is with their narrative structure. It is when the stories of the Christ Event and the beginnings of the church are placed in their proper order and context that they can confirm the truth of what Luke's readers have been instructed. Indeed, whereas Matthew follows Mark's outline to a great degree, Luke's narrative structure (although dependent on Mark for much of its content) is unique.

This means that any interpretation of Luke–Acts must pay close attention to the order of the materials in the narrative. Any interpretation of a piece of Luke–Acts must closely examine where it falls in the story line and how it relates to its narrative context. In other words, a key to understanding Luke's theology is understanding the narrative structure of Luke–Acts.

There is not, however, one clear outline to Luke–Acts. The author of the third gospel and Acts uses several techniques to structure the plot of his two-volume work, which give Luke–Acts a multileveled narrative structure. We will discuss three structural techniques that should influence any interpretation of the resurrection narrative.

Historical-Political Structure

First, Luke uses references to historical rulers to structure his plot chronologically (and politically). The beginning of the narrative has an explicit historical setting and time line in place. Luke begins his narrative of the Christ Event by telling of the miraculous conception of John the Baptist and dates the event in a typical fashion, that is, by referring to the ruler at the time of the story: "In the days of King Herod of Judea" (1:5). The date of Mary's pregnancy is then given in relation to Elizabeth's. She conceives Jesus six months after Elizabeth becomes pregnant (1:26). Three months after this, of course (1:56), Elizabeth gives birth to a son, who eight days later is circumcised and named (1:59). The readers know that Jesus is born approximately six months later, yet Luke gives a more precise dating, which on the one hand highlights Jesus' birth over John's and on the other explains why Jesus was born in Bethlehem instead of Nazareth:

> In those days a decree went out from Emperor Augustus that all the world should be registered. This was the first registration and was taken while Quirinius was governor of Syria. (2:1–2, NRSV)

Scholars have long recognized that this reference is probably not historically correct, but Luke's attempt to refer to two rulers and a specific census nevertheless shows his intent to ground his theological narrative in the historical world. As with John and in accordance with Jewish ritual practice, Jesus is circumcised and named eight days after being born (2:21). The only other story from Jesus' childhood is also dated precisely. It is at Passover twelve years later (2:41–42).

While most of the individual scenes in Luke–Acts are not dated as precisely as these opening ones, Luke does use such references here and there to give a sense of time progression that structures the story. When the story moves from Jesus' and John's births and childhoods to their adult ministries, Luke does not give a time reference relative to these earlier events (such as referring to Jesus' age) but offers the most detailed reference to rulers in the narrative:

In the fifteenth year of the reign of Emperor Tiberius, when Pontius Pilate was governor of Judea, and Herod was ruler [in all cases "ruler" is a translation of *tetrarch*] of Galilee, and his brother Philip ruler of the region of Ituraea and Trachonitis, and Lysanius ruler of Abilene, during the high priesthood of Annas and Caiaphas... (3:1–2, NRSV)

It is important to recognize how much Luke tells the readers in this short space. A new emperor is on the throne in Rome (as compared with Augustus in 2:1) and has been for fifteen years. And Herod's kingdom (1:5) has been divided among his heirs (who are now called tetrarchs instead of kings), with a Roman administrator serving as governor in Judea. In addition to the political dating, Luke offers a dating in relation to the temple authorities, Annas and Caiaphas. Later in the narrative, the reappearance of some of these local authorities (high priest– Lk. 22:54; Acts 4:6; Pilate–Lk. 13:1; 23:1; Herod [Antipas], tetrarch of Galilee–Lk. 3:19; 9:7; 23:7) shows that this dating covers the whole of Jesus' ministry as narrated in Luke and the beginning of the narrative of Acts.

The gospel narrative ends at the time of the "festival of Unleavened Bread, which is called the Passover" (22:1). Instead of offering a new date at the beginning of Acts, Luke simply uses relative dating. Jesus appears to the apostles for forty days after the resurrection before ascending into heaven (Acts 1:3; this conflicts with the ending of Luke, which presents Jesus as ascending on the evening following his resurrection (Lk. 24:51). The next explicit time reference is to Pentecost, the Jewish festival that takes place fifty days after Passover, so just a week or so after the Ascension (Acts 2:1). But as the story moves past this opening, precise dating is lacking. The scene after Pentecost opens with the ambiguous reference "One day..." (3:1). Clearly, the time that has passed is meant to be perceived as relatively short, since Annas and Caiaphas try Peter and John in 4:6 and Herod and Pontius Pilate are fresh in the apostles' memory, as seen in their speech in 4:27. And indeed, the high priest appears repeatedly in the rest of the first half of Acts without being named, leading the reader to presume that the position has not been passed on, that is, that the narrative is in the same basic temporal setting (Acts 5:17, 21, 27; 7:1; 9:1).

Although Luke never again offers a precise historical dating with reference to the political leaders of the day, in the second half of Acts new rulers begin appearing in the narrative and give the reader the sense of time passing. While modern readers may not be able to appreciate fully the significance of these references, Luke could have assumed that his original readers would have known of these rulers and their relative dates. A severe famine is mentioned as occurring "during the reign of Claudius" (Acts 11:28). In chapter 12 a new "Herod" persecutes the church in Judea and then is struck down by the angel of the Lord in Caesarea, the regional headquarters, for not deflecting deification. While Luke does not specify that this Herod is Agrippa, the title change from Herod the tetrarch in the gospel to "King Herod" (reminiscent of the Herod who appeared at the beginning of Luke's narrative, Lk. 1:5) indicates to the readers that he is speaking of a new ruler. Gallio, proconsul of Achaia, is presented in 18:12–17 as refusing to hear accusations against Paul because they have nothing to do with Roman law. Paul is tried before the Sanhedrin in Acts 22:30–23:10. At this trial, Ananias has replaced Annas and Caiaphas as the high priest (23:1–5). To keep Paul out of danger, he is taken to Caesarea where Felix now rules as governor over the territory (23:24–24:26). Paul stays in prison there for two years until Felix is succeeded by Porcius Festus (24:27). Festus invites King Agrippa, representing yet another generation of the Herodian family, to help him decide how to evaluate Paul's case (25:13–32). Festus and Agrippa have no choice, however, except to send Paul on to the emperor, because he chose to appeal to the emperor to escape being returned to Jerusalem for trial.

It is noteworthy that, with all these references to political leaders, the emperor at the end of the narrative is left unnamed, even though Paul's imminent appearance before him is mentioned several times (25:10–12, 21; 26:32; 27:24; 28:19). Nevertheless, by the time readers have worked from Luke 1:5 through Acts 25, they have a strong sense of the flow of history in relation to the story of the Christ Event and the beginnings of the church.

There are several possible implications to be drawn from this structural technique of Luke's that we should keep in mind when we turn our focus to the resurrection narrative. By linking the events that are narrated with the progression of political figures, the narrative implies that the story has political implications. Similarly, by presenting the events as taking place within history, the narrative implies that the story has historical implications. Luke's story, therefore, is a presentation of a salvation history that is linked with the political history of the Roman Empire. As such, it is not a presentation of an individual salvation that is otherworldly in character, but of a corporate salvation that is to be discovered *in* this world.

Geographical Structure

The second technique Luke uses to structure his theological narrative is a geographical schema. This schema is less evident when readers step up close to examine the individual brush strokes than it is when stepping back to see the picture as a whole. For example, in the opening chapters of the gospel the narrative jumps back and forth between Judea and Galilee numerous times. Likewise, in the accounts of Paul's missionary travels, the narrative moves from city to city and region to region in quick fashion, returning to some locations (including Jerusalem) several times on later trips while also advancing to new places.

But when we look at the narrative as a whole, a more unified geographical movement is noticeable. Following the introductory chapters, Jesus' ministry is focused in Galilee (Lk. 4:14–9:50). Luke then gathers many of Jesus' sayings material into a travel narrative (9:51–19:28) that begins with the words "When the days drew near for him to be taken up, he set his face to go to Jerusalem" (9:51). Throughout this section of the narrative, Luke reminds the readers often that Jesus is journeying toward Jerusalem (9:57; 10:38; 13:22; 14:25; 17:11; 18:31; 19:11, 28).

The narrative setting remains Jerusalem not only through the temple controversies, the passion, and the resurrection, but also through Pentecost, the beginnings of the Jerusalem church, and the persecution of the Jerusalem church (Lk. 19:41–Acts

8:1). At the beginning of the second volume, however, Jesus tells the apostles that they will be his witnesses "in Jerusalem, in all Judea and Samaria, and to the ends of the earth" (Acts 1:8). In some sense this calling to witness to the ends of the earth is fulfilled on Pentecost when Peter preaches to "Jews from every nation under heaven," those who were "Parthian, Medes, Elamites, and residents of Mesopotamia, Judea and Cappadocia, Pontus and Asia, Phrygia and Pamphylia, Egypt and the parts of Libya belonging to Cyrene, and visitors from Rome...Cretans and Arabs" (2:5, 9–11). But the calling is also worked out throughout the narrative. When persecution breaks out in Jerusalem following Stephen's execution, Christians are scattered throughout "the countryside of Judea and Samaria" (8:1). Following an account of the conversion and baptism of some in Samaria (8:4–24), Luke tells of Philip's converting and baptizing a court official from Ethiopia (8:26–39). The readers can assume that the message of Jesus as the Messiah went with the official when he returned to Ethiopia (i.e., to another end of the earth). Luke's hinting at the spread of the gospel in other directions in this fashion allows him to focus on the spread counter-clockwise around the Mediterranean Sea, from Jerusalem to Rome. Indeed, in the next chapter, the readers witness the conversion of Saul/Paul, who will be presented as primarily responsible for the spread of the gospel in this fashion.

After becoming anchored in Antioch of Syria, which is north of Galilee (11:25–26), Paul's missionary trips take him west into Asia Minor and then into Europe (Acts 13–14; 16–19). In chapter 21, Paul returns to Jerusalem, where he gets into trouble in the temple. He remains under arrest for the rest of the narrative, and beginning in 25:10 it becomes clear that he will go to Rome to appear before the emperor, thus taking the gospel to "the end of the earth." Indeed, while the narrative ends without the trial before the emperor occurring, the last note of the text says that Paul was in Rome for two years "proclaiming the kingdom of God and teaching about the Lord Jesus Christ with all boldness and without hindrance" (28:31).

This geographical structure has much significance for those wanting to focus on the resurrection. Jerusalem is the geographical hinge of the narrative, of the salvation history. In the first volume everything moves toward Jerusalem. In the second volume everything moves out from Jerusalem. Thus, the passion and resurrection narrative is the center of the story, indeed the center of Luke's salvation history. The death and resurrection of Jesus are not just points in a linear view of history. They mark the key point toward which everything before heads and from which everything afterward proceeds. Luke's view of the resurrection can be read as summing up history and starting up history all at the same time.

Prophetic Pattern Structure

The third technique Luke uses to structure his two-volume narrative is a prophetic characterization pattern. This is a quite complicated pattern to which we cannot do justice in this short essay. Instead, we will attempt to offer a summary that is appropriate for our purposes.

A key to understanding this prophetic pattern is found in Deuteronomy 18:15 (see also v. 18), which is quoted in Peter's speech in Acts 3:22 and Stephen's speech in 7:37: "God will raise up [Gk. *anastesei*] a prophet for you from your own people as he raised me up." Obviously, for Luke, Jesus is this prophet raised up like Moses (notice the double meaning: Not only does God call a prophet to follow in the footsteps of Moses, but Jesus is literally "raised up" following the crucifixion). Luke had already hinted at this understanding of Jesus in the gospel by having Moses appear at the transfiguration with Elijah to discuss the "exodus" Jesus is to fulfill in Jerusalem (Lk. 9:30–31).

While scholars have looked at minute segments of the narrative for parallels between Jesus and Moses, we are primarily concerned with broad strokes. When we look for such, what we find is that Luke's story of Jesus' passion, resurrection, and ascension is reminiscent of elements of the story of the exodus. As Israel is persecuted by and suffers at the hand of Pharaoh, so Jesus is rejected by and suffers at the hands of the Jerusalem crowd, Jewish leaders, Pilate, and Herod because of Judas' betrayal (Lk. 22:2–23:56). As Israel is liberated by God, so is Jesus rescued from the tomb (24:1–7). As the Israelites slowly come to recognize the hand of God in the plagues and the exodus, so the disciples slowly recognize God's work in the empty tomb and the resurrection (24:11–12, 15–32, 37). As Pharaoh receives retribution by dying in the Red Sea, thus removing the threat of further persecution to Israel, so Judas dies a horrible death, which the reader is inclined to attribute to divine punishment because it fulfills scripture (Acts 1:16–20), and thus removes the possibility that he will betray his fellow apostles. And as Moses departs from the Israelites before they enter the promised land, so Jesus ascends to the heavens before the gift of the Holy Spirit is received by the apostles (Lk. 24:51; Acts 1:9–11). This Mosaic pattern of characterizing Jesus demonstrates that the Christ Event is linked with God's acts of salvation in Israel's sacred history. In other words, Luke's prophetic structure argues that God has not changed strategies in the middle of the game (as many Christians interpret the Christ Event). Jesus' death, resurrection, and ascension are both unique to him and stereotypical examples of God's work in the world. The providential plan of God revealed in Israel's ancient history is still playing itself out in the person of Jesus Christ.

Indeed, the eternal plan of God also plays itself out in the story of the church, for not only is Jesus patterned on the story of Moses and the exodus, but the prophetic pattern extends into Acts. Readers encounter the story of the exodus of Moses and the passion, resurrection, and ascension of Jesus recharacterized and reformulated in the stories of the major protagonists in the second half of Luke's story. This pattern occurs at key points in the story, serving as a transition from one narrative section to the next. Let us look at Stephen and Peter.

- As Jesus is persecuted and suffers, Stephen is stoned by the crowd (Acts 6:11–14; 7:57–58); and James is killed with the sword by Herod, who then arrests Peter during the Festival of Unleavened Bread to kill him also (12:1–4).
- As Jesus is resurrected, Stephen receives a vision of the glory of God and Jesus at God's right hand

(Acts 7:55–56), and Peter is rescued from prison by the angel of the Lord (Acts 12:6–11).

- As the disciples slowly recognize God's hand at work in Jesus' resurrection, Saul comes around to recognize the truth of Stephen's message (Acts 9:1–19; 22:3–21); and the crowd at the house of John Mark's mother slowly moves from doubt to recognition that Peter has indeed been freed (Acts 12:12–16).

- As Jesus' ascension removes him from the narrative, making way for the next plot movement to begin, Stephen's death (and presumed acceptance into Jesus' hands) removes him from the narrative and effects the spread of the gospel beyond Judea into Samaria (Acts 7:56–8:1); and James's death and Peter's leaving and going to another place (presumably on the lam, Acts 12:2, 17) removes the Twelve from center focus and allows the narrative to concentrate on Paul.

- And as Judas dies a horrible death and no longer represents a threat to the apostles, Saul, who approvingly witnessed Stephen's execution, is blinded and told he will suffer for Jesus' name and thus is no longer a persecutor (Acts 9:3–8, 16); and Herod, who has reduced the Twelve to eleven (with one in hiding), is struck down by the angel of the Lord for accepting deifying praise (Acts 12:20–24), thus ending another source of persecution.

The completion of the pattern with each Lukan character (Jesus–Stephen–Peter) moves the narrative forward in a dramatic fashion. Following Jesus' passion, resurrection, and ascension, the establishment of the church in Jerusalem by the Twelve moves to center stage. Following the stoning and vision of Stephen, the spread of the gospel beyond Jerusalem takes central position. Following the death of James and the arrest, escape, and flight of Peter, the spread of the gospel to the ends of the earth by Paul becomes the primary focus.

This literary pattern also establishes a theological structure for a Christian understanding of history. We have already noted that this prophetic pattern is grounded in the past by echoing the story of Moses. Similarly, Luke indicates that the providential plan of God will continue into the future by extending the prophetic pattern to Paul but ending the narrative without drawing the pattern to a close. Like Jesus, Paul travels to Jerusalem (Acts 20:16–21:17), is arrested, rejected by the crowds (21:27–22:22), and tried (and declared innocent) by a Roman ruler and a member of the Herodian lineage (25:1–26:32). The persecution and rejection set the stage for the pattern of suffering, rescue, removal from the story, and retribution. But the narrative ends with Paul under house arrest in Rome waiting to be tried by the emperor (28:16, 19). Readers are left to assume that as the pattern has held true in the past, so will it continue through the story of Paul. Indeed, the fact that the emperor is left unnamed allows readers to interpret the open ending in such a way as to recognize the pattern extending into their own history. As they face persecution and suffering analogous to that about which they have read, the readers of Luke–Acts can also hope for resurrection and retribution analogous to that which they have read. God's providential plan extends from Moses to Jesus, through Stephen, Peter, and Paul, to the readers.

Indeed, this pattern plays a significant role in addressing the theological issue of the delay of the parousia, which many scholars have argued is the primary problem Luke is attempting to address. The argument goes like this: Luke writes late in the first century, when Christians have begun to lose hope (or perhaps have long lost hope) that Christ will return soon. Luke changes the early kerygmatic eschatology into a form of realized eschatology to make sense of an ongoing history of the movement that began with Jesus. Luke makes many literary, rhetorical, and theological moves to show that a delayed parousia does not imply that the good news of Jesus Christ's gospel is null and void, but study of these techniques is beyond our scope. It is important for us to note, however, that this prophetic pattern supports this move by extending the pattern of the Christ Event into the time of the apostles and of the readers. At the same time that Luke historicizes the passion and resurrection, he also makes it contemporary.

Summary

Luke's displeasure with the narrative order of the stories in his sources led him to create a multilayered order structured on political history, geography, and prophetic characterization. While these new narrative structures, folded into one narrative, have literary significance, their primary importance is theological. In terms of our focus on the resurrection narrative, the politicohistorical structure indicates that the resurrection does not have an otherworldly focus. It speaks about salvation and rescue in this life. The geographical structure, which places Jerusalem, and thus the resurrection, at the center of the narrative, indicates that the resurrection should occupy the center of Christian theological reflection. As it is the hinge of the Lukan story, so is the resurrection the hinge of the Christian worldview. Finally, the prophetic pattern, which extends back to Moses and forward to the readers, indicates that resurrection is part of God's providential plan not just for Jesus and the earliest Christians but for all of history. Resurrection/salvation is not a past historical event, but a historically established pattern that is open for readers to experience.

Lukan Characters Interpret the Resurrection

The fact that Luke writes a story that includes both the Christ Event and the Church Event (if you will) affords the interpreter an opportunity not available when reading Mark or Matthew. The fact that the story of the Church Event extends past that of the Christ Event allows the author to reflect explicitly on the previous part of the narrative in a manner inappropriate in the midst of narrating the events in Jesus' life, death, and resurrection themselves. Indeed, Acts has numerous speeches in which apostles and others preach that Jesus is the Christ by anchoring their claim on an interpretation of the resurrection. Therefore, before we turn to the resurrection narrative itself, we should note the ways these characters interpret the resurrection in the context of Luke's narrative of the beginnings of the church as a final means of preparing us to hear in the resurrection narrative what Luke uniquely offers.

In the speeches in Acts, the resurrection is repeatedly placed in contrast with the actions of those who rejected Jesus. When the narrative is set in Jerusalem, the formula is "*You* killed Jesus, but *God* raised him…" (Acts 2:23–24; 3:15; 4:10; 5:30). Even when the setting is moved outside Jerusalem, the contrast is still emphasized by adjusting the formula to "*they* killed, *God* raised" (Acts 10:39–40; 13:27–30). While it was necessary (Gk. *dei*) for Jesus to suffer as part of God's providential plan (e.g., see Lk. 9:22; 13:33; 17:25; 24:7, 26; Acts 2:23; 17:3), the contrast places responsibility for Jesus' death on those in Jerusalem while explicitly claiming that the resurrection was a divine action. Indeed, Luke makes two significant redactional changes to Mark that indicate the crucifixion was a necessary martyrdom, but was not in itself an act of salvation: (1) Luke omits Mark 10:45 in which Jesus states, "For the Son of Man came not to be served but to serve, and to give his life a ransom for many." (2) Unlike in Mark and Matthew, when Jesus dies on the cross, the centurion does not recognize him as God's Son (Mk. 15:39; Mt. 27:54) but instead says, "Certainly this man was innocent" (23:47).

Therefore, in Luke–Acts the resurrection and not the passion is the crux of salvation. It is by faith in the name of the risen Jesus Christ that healings are performed by the apostles (Acts 3:16; 4:9–12). It is Jesus' resurrection that confirms that there will be a general resurrection (Acts 4:2; 23:6; 24:15, 21). And finally, it is through the resurrection that Jesus has been exalted to a position to judge and forgive:

- God exalted him at his right hand as Leader and Savior, that he might give repentance to Israel and forgiveness of sins. (Acts 5:31)

- They put him to death by hanging him on a tree; but God raised him on the third day and allowed him to appear, not to all the people but to us who were chosen by God as witnesses, and who ate and drank with him after he rose from the dead. He commanded us to preach to the people and to testify that he is the one ordained by God as judge of the living and the dead. All the prophets testify about him that everyone who believes in him receives forgiveness of sins through his name. (Acts 10:39–43)

- He whom God raised up experienced no corruption. Let it be known to you therefore, my brothers, that through this man forgiveness of sins is proclaimed to you; by this Jesus everyone who believes is set free from all those sins from which you could not be freed by the law of Moses. Beware, therefore, that what the prophets said does not happen to you: "Look, you scoffers! Be amazed and perish, for in your days I am doing a work, a work that you will never believe, even if someone tells you." (Acts 13:37–41)

- While God has overlooked the times of human ignorance, now he commands all people everywhere to repent, because he has fixed a day on which he will have the world judged in righteousness by a man whom he has appointed, and of this he has given assurance to all by raising him from the dead. (Acts 17:30–31)

Truly, for Luke–Acts the resurrection is the hinge upon which everything else swings. It not only serves simultaneously as the end of the story of the Christ Event and the beginning of the story of the Church Event, but it is central to any understanding of salvation and is the key to christology. With all this aid, we are finally prepared to turn to the resurrection narrative itself.

The Resurrection Narrative

Following Mark, Luke has Joseph of Arimathea bury Jesus, but Luke goes even further than Matthew in removing from Joseph any possible guilt in the Sanhedrin's condemnation of Jesus. The narrator describes him as "a good and righteous man…who, though a member of the council, had not agreed to their plan and action" (Lk. 23:50–51). The fact, therefore, that the women who have followed Jesus from Galilee see that his body is in need of further treatment does not imply a scandal (23:55–56). Luke simply follows Mark's technique in getting the women to the tomb on the morning of the first day of the week.

Indeed, in Luke 24:1–12 the Lukan narrator follows the bulk of Mark's version of the scene at the empty tomb fairly closely (see Mk. 16:1–8). The changes in some of the details, however, are extremely significant. The women arrive at dawn with spices to anoint Jesus' body. Luke deletes Mark's reference to the women's concern about how to move the stone away from the entrance to the tomb, but nevertheless the stone is moved when the women arrive (Lk. 24:1–2). The women puzzle over the absence of Jesus' body, not recognizing the empty tomb as a sign that Jesus has been raised (24:3).

While they stand there perplexed, suddenly two men appear to be standing by them who are going to make the connection between the empty tomb and the resurrection explicit for them (Lk. 24:4). But who are these "two men"? Mark's messenger at the tomb was the "young man" from the arrest scene (Mk. 14:51; 16:5). Like Matthew, Luke omits the reference to the young man running away naked as Jesus is arrested, so a substitute is needed at the tomb. Instead of utilizing an angel as did Matthew, however, Luke makes the connection between the empty tomb scene and the transfiguration even stronger than it was in Mark (see the discussion in Markan exegesis section above). In Luke 9, Jesus is transfigured so that his clothes become dazzlingly white (Gk. *leukos exastrapton*, v. 29), and the appearance of Moses and Elijah is described in this fashion:

> Suddenly they saw two men [Gk. *andres duo*], Moses and Elijah, talking to him. They appeared in glory and were speaking of his departure [Gk. *exodon*], which he was about to accomplish at Jerusalem. (Lk. 9:30–31, NRSV)

Luke has added to Mark's account of the transfiguration the reference to Jesus' exodus to Jerusalem, making clear that this scene is to be read as foreshadowing what will be read in the Jerusalem narrative. When the description of the two men (Gk. *andres duo*) wearing dazzling clothes (Gk. *astraptouse*) at the empty tomb echoes the language of the transfiguration, the connection is drawn all the tighter (Lk. 24:4). Indeed, the connection is close enough to question whether these two men at the tomb are not Moses and Elijah themselves.

As with the women in Mark's version, the women at the tomb in Luke's story are frightened by this epiphany. But unlike Mark's characters, these women move past this initial fear. The two men remind the women that Jesus has declared the divine necessity of his suffering, death, *and* resurrection and question why they would be there seeking Jesus in the first place (Lk. 24:5–7). Immediately remembering Jesus' words, the women leave the tomb, and instead of being too afraid to tell anyone what they had seen and heard, as in Mark 16:8, they "told all this to the eleven and to all the rest" (Lk. 24:8–9).

Luke, however, does not remove the scandal from the empty tomb; he simply displaces it. It is the apostles instead of the women who are not initially open to the proclamation of Jesus' resurrection. When the women tell them what they have experienced at the tomb, "these words seemed to them [the apostles] an idle tale, and they did not believe them" (24:10–11). And, of course, unlike Mark, Luke moves on to work through the scandal within the narrative instead of leaving it for the readers to resolve.

But Luke's is an intriguing resolution. Luke does not immediately proceed to affirming the witness of the women by having the risen Jesus appear to the apostles. Instead, Jesus appears (without being initially recognized) to two disciples who have not had a role in the narrative before and who are unknown to the readers—unless, of course, Cleopas, the only one of the two travelers to Emmaus who is named, was known to Luke's original community of readers (Lk. 24:13–35).

The fact that these two disciples are heading to Emmaus, which Luke notes is about seven miles from Jerusalem, shows that the group of disciples who followed Jesus and who witnessed his crucifixion (see Lk. 23:49) are already breaking apart and failing to trust in the promise/prophecy of Jesus' resurrection. If the Holy Spirit is to come upon those in the city, Luke must bring the disciples back together. As the two disciples are walking along discussing the events of the past days, Jesus joins them and walks with them, but they do not recognize him (24:16). Again, we see that the gospel writer's image of the resurrected Jesus is not simply a bodily resurrection. Close followers "are kept from recognizing him," implying a different appearance on Jesus' part. Indeed, their failure to know that their companion is Jesus emphasizes again that the disciples, even after having heard from the women that Jesus has been raised, have not believed Jesus' own prediction of his fate. They are not looking for a risen Jesus.

This lack of recognition, of course, allows Luke to shape a scene full of irony. The readers know that Jesus is talking about himself, but the disciples think they are having a third-person conversation. Jesus "plays dumb" and asks what the disciples are discussing. They recount, in summary fashion, all that has happened, making explicit the fact that their hopes have been dashed by the crucifixion:

> …Jesus of Nazareth, who was a prophet mighty in deed and word before God and all the people, and how our chief priests and leaders handed him over to be condemned to death and crucified him. But we had hoped that he was the one to redeem Israel. Yes, and besides all this, it is now the third day since these things took place. Moreover, some women of our group astounded us. They were at the tomb early this morning, and when they did not find his body there, they came back and told us that they had indeed seen a vision of angels who said that he was alive. Some of those who were with us went to the tomb and found it just as the women had said; but they did not see him. (Lk. 24:19–24, NRSV)

But their recitation of the recent events falls short of understanding the significance of those events. In other words, they know the story but are unable to interpret it. This task of interpretation is left for the risen and hidden Jesus. He makes clear that all that had happened was of divine necessity as foretold by the scriptures (Lk. 24:25–27). But even this does not reveal to the disciples the identity of their companion.

It is only when Jesus, invited to stay and eat with the two disciples, blesses and breaks bread in a fashion that recalls the Last Supper that they recognize him. The moment they do, he vanishes (again showing that Jesus' resurrection did not simply raise him to his earlier bodily existence, Lk. 24:28b–31). At that point the disciples recall that their hearts had burned within them as Jesus had interpreted the scriptures for them (24:32). While the narrator is concerned with asserting that Jesus' death and resurrection were part of God's providential plan, he is also clearly concerned in this scene with defining one of the ways that the risen Christ is still present with the community of faith. While Christ's presence is not always recognized and indeed seems fleeting, it is in the interpretation of scripture and sacramental practice that this presence is revealed.

In case we are too comfortable asserting that Luke presents Jesus' resurrection as something other than bodily, in the next scene Jesus' bodily presence is emphasized as part of resurrection theology. The two disciples return from Emmaus to tell of their experience, only to discover that Peter too has seen the risen Jesus, though this appearance is not directly narrated (24:33–35). (In contrast with their consideration of the women's report as an idle tale, the Eleven now are willing to accept that Jesus is risen because a male apostle offers testimony: "The Lord has risen indeed, and he has appeared to Simon!" 24:34.) As they are speaking, Jesus appears to the whole group, and yet they still question whether they are seeing a spirit (24:36–37). So Luke presents Jesus as relieving their doubts by showing his wounds to them and by eating in front of them (24:38–43). Jesus then interprets his passion and resurrection in light of scripture for the whole group, as he had for the two disciples on the road (24:44–49). At this point, his words also begin to foreshadow events and emphases in Acts. Jesus' resurrection should lead to the proclamation of repentance and forgiveness of sins to all nations, beginning in Jerusalem. And the resurrection allows for the sending of the promise, power from on high–that is, the Holy Spirit.

Indeed, in Luke the resurrection narrative cannot be separated from the stories of the ascension and Pentecost. Liturgically, the church has followed the chronology of Acts 1–2 in separating Easter from Ascension Day and Pentecost by forty and fifty days. But in Luke–Acts the chronology does not imply separate theological meanings. Indeed in the gospel, even as the closing passages foreshadow the opening of Acts, the ascension takes place immediately after the resurrection appearance just described (Lk. 24:50–53). Jesus shows the disciples his wounds, eats in front of them, interprets the passion and resurrection in light of the scriptures, leads them out to Bethany, and ascends into heaven. The short span of time in the gospel signals the reader to understand the story of the ascension in Acts as being part and parcel of the resurrection story. This close linking is made stronger by the reappearance of the two men who had spoken to the women at the tomb. Following Jesus' being lifted up, two men dressed in white (again recalling the connection to the transfiguration) ask a question similar to the one asked of the women at the tomb: "Men of Galilee, why do you stand looking up toward heaven? This Jesus, who has been taken up from you into heaven, will come in the same way as you saw him go into heaven" (Acts 1:10–11).

For Luke, the problem with writing a narrative that extends from Jesus' birth to Paul's awaiting trial in Rome is how to get Jesus off the stage. Because Mark and Matthew ended their stories with the resurrection, they did not confront this problem. But in terms of plot and theology, Luke is forced to answer the question, If Jesus was raised, where is he now? The ascension, as exaltation to God's right hand, removes Jesus from the narrative and opens up the possibility of continuing with a new story angle. But the story of the ascension then raises the subsequent question of Jesus' absence: When will Jesus return? Indeed, the words of the two men concerning Jesus' "coming in the same way" seems to point to a high expectation of the parousia. Luke's answer to this question, however, is the story of Pentecost. The rush of the wind from heaven and the tongues of fire resting on each of those gathered in the one place lead to their being filled with the Holy Spirit. The Holy Spirit is the presence of the risen Jesus Christ, albeit experienced in a new manner, after the visible Jesus has ascended. The resurrection, with its ambiguity concerning Jesus' physicality, allows this narrative, theological claim of Jesus' continuing presence to be made.

Those preaching Luke's version of the Easter story are challenged to present a vision of the presence of the risen Christ in a manner that is faithful to Luke's understanding of the Holy Spirit as well as to Luke's presentation of Jerusalem (where both the resurrection and Pentecost take place) as the center of the Christ–Church Event. Luke could be read as saying that through the gift of the Holy Spirit we are included in the prophetic pattern and should expect to participate in the resurrection of Jesus Christ as the central salvific experience of our lives.

This experience should not be thought of as a one-time conversion experience of some sort, but as ongoing revelation for people of faith. Luke's mythic pattern of divine rescue gives meaning to all those times in life where divine goodness confronts the many forms of evil in the world. Indeed, this confrontation should never be perceived as final. The very structure of Luke–Acts demonstrates that there are recurring defeats and victories, recurring crucifixion and resurrection, throughout our lives, and indeed throughout human existence.

Luke does not simply leave this issue at the level of narrative commentary on the readers' experience of crucifixion and resurrection in their own lives. In the resurrection narrative, he provides the church with a way to concretely symbolize that pattern of existence. Jesus' interpretation of scripture and breaking of the bread models a service of word and table. As his interpretation of scripture makes clear, Jesus' crucifixion was of divine necessity. On the other hand, so was the resurrection. Indeed, while the Last Supper establishes the sacrament of the Lord's Supper as a meal recalling the crucifixion, the risen Jesus' being revealed in the breaking of bread is a symbol of the risen Christ's presence with Luke's readers in the eucharist. In other words, as at the center of the Luke–Acts narrative stands the death and resurrection of Jesus, so at the center of the life of the church stands worship, which in turn models and reveals the fact that at the center of the Christian's life stands the pattern of death and resurrection, where the presence of Christ is found.

Eucharist (Lk. 24:13–49)

When United Methodists share this meal together in the context of worship, we usually call it either the *Lord's supper* or *holy communion.* They are both fine, decent labels that describe different elements of the significance of the meal.

The label *Lord's supper* reminds us that Jesus, at his last supper, commanded that this meal be shared in remembrance of him. The bread and wine re-member the body and blood of Christ that was given on our behalf–the body that was nailed to the cross and the blood that poured out from his wounds. With this emphasis, it is no wonder that receiving the Lord's supper is so often a solemn, quiet, reflective experience. It evokes sorrow concerning the state of a world that would kill God's only begotten Child. It evokes penitence concerning our individual, sinful participation in the brokenness of the world. And it evokes silent awe concerning the ultimate expression of self-giving love that is represented by the cross.

The label *holy communion*, on the other hand, points to the connection that exists among those of us who share this meal. The root of communion is *common*. And, of course, what we have in common is Jesus Christ. In the early church, it was only after a convert was baptized into the name of Jesus that she or he could partake in this sacrament. Nonbaptized people could attend Christian worship in which the Word was proclaimed, but only the baptized were allowed into holy communion. Many churches still hold baptism as a requirement for receiving communion. We United Methodists, however, celebrate an open table to which everyone is welcome. This does not mean that we disregard the communal element of the sacrament. To the contrary, we strongly emphasize it; we simply do so in a different manner than did the early church or than do some of our fellow Christians. We claim that Christ invites all to this table and that is what we all have in common. Not that we have all been baptized into Christ, but that we are all invited by Christ. To be especially tautological, what we all have in common is communion with Christ.

So important aspects of the meaningfulness of this sacrament are indicated by these two labels, *Lord's supper* and *holy communion*. But if we only use these two labels, we leave out another central part of the significance of the sacrament, an element that is especially called to our attention during the season of Easter. So today, I want us to lay aside the familiar labels (not discard, just lay aside) and pick up another label that we all know but just don't use very often. Today I want us to celebrate the sacrament of the *eucharist*.

The Greek root of *eucharist* means to give thanks. So every time we share this sacrament and pray the Great Thanksgiving, we are performing a eucharistic act, whether we call it that or not. And, indeed, every time we talk of *celebrating* this sacrament, we are talking in eucharistic terms. The problem is, of course, that we don't usually celebrate when we share this meal. There is very little celebration as we wait for the ushers to tell us when we are allowed to silently process forward, then kneel in silent prayer as we are given the elements, and finally return to our pews in silence where we wait for everyone else to finish up so that we can sing the final hymn and go home. We may feel thankful, but it's not a loud, celebratory, eucharistic thankfulness; it's a quiet, solemn thankfulness that is appropriate for the Lord's supper.

There's an old story of an evangelist who was the guest preacher at a very formal church one Sunday. At one point in his sermon, he had almost everyone rolling on the floor laughing at what he was saying. But after the service, one woman who had *not* been laughing approached him and commented on the inappropriateness of such humor in the context of sacred worship. The preacher responded by saying, "Madam, we should never confuse religion with a stomachache." I must say that sometimes when we share this meal, I wonder if it causes us all indigestion. We are *so* quiet and stiff. Surely there is something here to celebrate; surely there is reason to offer a loud, joyous "Thank you!"

I suspect that after the crucifixion, Jesus' followers had their own share of upset stomachs. Our digestive systems are often messed up in periods of stress and grief. I can imagine that as Cleopas and his friend head out of Jerusalem, they do so with some measure of discomfort, with their hands on their bellies as they walk. After all, even as they leave to get away, they carry on the conversation about hopes that have been dashed, about a loved one who has been taken from them, and—of all things—about a missing body.

Perhaps it is their stomachaches that keep their eyes from seeing Jesus when he appears to them. Perhaps it is their pain that keeps them from realizing that it is Jesus who is interpreting scripture for them, who is prophetically interpreting what is going on in the world around them. And maybe that's why they only finally recognize Jesus when they go inside and sit down at table to satisfy their stomachs. It is when Jesus takes the bread, blesses it, and breaks it that they suddenly realize that it is Christ who is in their midst. And as soon as they realize it, Jesus disappears. But that brief glimpse evokes a joy that they describe in terms of their hearts burning within them. (Do you suppose they were Methodists—you know, the whole "heart strangely warmed" thing?)

Anyway, that's what this meal, as the eucharist, is all about. It's about celebrating, about giving thanks for the presence of Christ. Let's be clear. It's not about the presence of Christ in the bread or in the wine; it's not even about the presence of Christ in the act of sharing the meal, although Christ might be present in both of those ways. The eucharistic celebration gives thanks that the presence of the risen Christ is the presence of the one who *had* to die. In other words, we don't celebrate some warm, fuzzy kind of presence. As the resurrection reversed the crucifixion, so the presence of the risen Christ is found in places where reversal is taking place in today's world: in moments of salvation where the mighty are thrown down and the lowly are lifted up. As eucharist, this meal doesn't point to something way back then, nor does it point to itself inside this sanctuary. It points to the presence of Jesus Christ being revealed *out there, right now.*

I think I first became aware of the need for United Methodists to embrace a more eucharistic approach to this meal when I was on staff at Trinity United Methodist Church in Atlanta, Georgia. Trinity is a church that has long had a deep concern for the homeless in downtown Atlanta. Every Sunday they provide a noontime meal for whoever wants one. The problem the church has always experienced is that, while the congregation is inside worshiping, these homeless men, women, and children are standing outside in line waiting to be fed. Over and over again they were invited inside to join us for worship or even just to come into the narthex to stay warm until the food was served. But only a few would ever come. Most wanted to stay as close to the front of the line as possible.

The worship committee finally decided to take worship out to them one Sunday. They wanted to be very careful that this didn't turn into one of those settings where you must first listen to a sermon before you are fed. So what we did was take communion out to the line. We were very careful to offer people the opportunity to participate without pressuring them or making them feel awkward if they didn't wish to. We had predicted that only a few would participate, but to our surprise most did.

But it was not a silent, solemn partaking of the Lord's supper or holy communion. It was a boisterous, loud eucharist. There was joking about whether or not the chalice contained real wine. Some were quite disappointed to discover Welch's grape juice. One woman, after she had taken the bread and juice and we had already moved down the line, started singing "Amazing Grace." And I'll never forget this one man who was toward the front of the line and seemed to be very confrontational with the other people in the line around him, as if he was really having to exert himself to protect his place in the line. I assumed he wouldn't have any interest in us, but we asked him nevertheless whether he wished to be served communion. At that point he stepped out of the line with a sort of mischievous sparkle in his eye and a half grin and said, "Oh, I never turn down the body and blood of my Lord." And when he took the dipped bread into his mouth, while his mouth was still full, he uttered a loud, "Thank you, Jesus," and laughed a deep belly laugh.

Then our eyes were opened and we recognized Christ in our presence. And we said to one another, "Were not our hearts burning within us while Christ was talking to us in the parking lot?" That same hour we got up and returned to the sanctuary and found our companions gathered together. They were saying, "Christ has risen and appeared to us!" Then we told what had happened in the parking lot, and how Christ had been made known to us in the breaking of the bread, how Christ had been made known to us in the eucharist.

CHAPTER 5

Resurrection in the Gospel of John: Easter Reordered

The Gospel According to John ends (20:30–31)...and then it ends again (21:1–25). Scholars have long debated whether the final chapter is an epilogue from the hand of the original author or an addition provided by a later redactor. Regardless, there is no ancient manuscript of John's narrative that ends with chapter 20, so the "epilogue" deserves to be read not only as part of the whole work but indeed as a major part of the resurrection narrative. Therefore, John's readers are offered the opportunity to reflect on the meaning of the resurrection from more than one angle.

John presents a radically different interpretation of the Christ Event than do Mark, Matthew, and Luke. When placed next to the synoptics, several broad, unique features are evident.

First, *John's time line is different.* Jesus goes to Judea numerous times instead of only once; his ministry lasts three years instead of one; and Jesus is crucified on the Day of Preparation instead of on the first day of Passover.

Second, *John utilizes different types of material.* Instead of speaking in short parables about the dominion of God, Jesus delivers lengthy christological discourses. Instead of narrating the conflict between Jesus and the Jewish authorities in short controversy stories, John presents long dramatic and dialogical scenes. The voices of Jesus and the narrator get intertwined to the point of being almost indistinguishable at times. And most of the material in John is not found in the synoptics, nor is much synoptic material found in John.

Third, *John's theology is very different.* The incarnation of the preexistent One, including specifically Jesus' special relation to God, replaces the advent of the dominion of God as the central emphasis of the good news.

And while John's resurrection narrative does follow the basic pattern found in the synoptic gospels–the women's visit to the empty tomb followed by appearances of the risen Jesus to the disciples (even Mark, who does narrate resurrection appearances, assumes this structure)–there are a number of elements in John's two chapters dealing with the resurrection that are unique to the Fourth Gospel. The risen Jesus appears to Mary Magdalene but does not allow her to hold him. The risen Jesus appears to Thomas, who does not have faith that he has risen, and invites him to touch his wounds. The risen Jesus appears to the disciples in both Jerusalem *and* Galilee. The risen Jesus performs a miracle by effecting the large catch of fish. Finally, the risen Jesus questions Peter concerning the apostle's love for him, instructs Peter to feed his sheep, and foreshadows Peter's martyrdom. Moreover, it is within the context of the resurrection narratives that John defines the purpose of his gospel:

> Now Jesus did many other signs in the presence of his disciples, which are not written in this book. But these are written so that you may come to believe that Jesus is the Messiah, the Son of God, and that through believing you may have life in his name. (20:30–31, NRSV)

Therefore, when we preach John's Easter story, we should have something (indeed many things) quite different to say than when we preach on one of the synoptics' resurrection narratives, and what we say should express the heart of John's gospel.

Resurrection in the Context of John's Narrative

Although there are many subtle transitions in the plot of the Fourth Gospel, a major transition takes place between chapters 12 and 13. In the first half of the narrative, it is clear that Jesus' hour to be glorified has not yet arrived (2:4; 7:6, 8,

30, 39; 8:20). But just after he enters Jerusalem for the last time, Jesus chooses not to meet some Greeks who are seeking him because his hour to be glorified has arrived (12:23). This recognition is repeated quickly in 13:1, at which point Jesus turns from a public ministry to a private engagement of his disciples. This major transition has led many commentators to speak of John as consisting of two "books": the Book of Signs (chaps. 1–12) and the Book of Glory (chaps. 13–20, with chap. 21 being an epilogue). Although this division is overly simplistic, it does offer some helpful insight into much of the Johannine material. During his public ministry, Jesus reveals his identity to his own through speech and sign, only to be rejected. When his hour arrives, Jesus' glory is revealed to those who accept him through his passion, resurrection, ascension, and gift of the Paraclete.

The second half of the gospel can be divided into three parts: the farewell discourse (chaps. 13–17), the passion narrative (18–19), and the resurrection narrative (20–21). The resurrection stories in chapters 20–21 are, of course, the culmination of the entire gospel, but the farewell discourse and the passion narrative prepare the reader to encounter the resurrection in unique ways.

Farewell Discourse

In chapters 13–17 Jesus washes the disciples' feet, offers them his final teaching during the Last Supper, and prays on their behalf. While this long scene clearly sets the stage for Jesus' arrest and crucifixion, it also foreshadows the resurrection in many significant ways.

- Repeatedly in this section, the readers are told that Jesus is going to depart from this world and return to the Father (13:1, 3, 33, 36; 14:2–5, 18–19, 28; 16:5, 7, 10, 16–19, 28; 17:11, 13). Therefore, the readers are prepared to understand the resurrection and ascension as part of the departure (along with the crucifixion).

- Throughout the Fourth Gospel there is a heavy emphasis on having faith (in the NRSV the Greek noun *pistis* is usually translated as "faith," not "belief," but the verb *pisteuo* is usually translated as "believe," since there is no English verb form of "faith"). This is true as well in the farewell discourse (13:19; 14:1, 10–12, 29; 16:9, 27, 30–31; 17:8, 20–21). This foreshadows Jesus' interchange with Thomas concerning believing and seeing (20:27–29) as well as John's declaration of the purpose of the gospel's being that the readers might come to have faith (20:31).

• After washing the disciples' feet, Jesus instructs them to do as he has done, for servants are not greater than their master (13:12–17; see also 15:27; 17:18). And indeed, when the risen Jesus appears to the disciples, he sends them out as the Father has sent him (20:21), and he calls Peter to "follow" him (21:19).

• The disciple whom Jesus loved first appears during the farewell scene when the disciples are questioning who will betray Jesus (13:23–25). He is mentioned alongside Peter (v. 24), and indeed the two of them are paired in the resurrection narratives (20:3–10; 21:7, 20–23).

• Jesus issues the new commandment to his disciples to love one another in 13:24–35 and again in 15:12–17 (see also 17:26). Similarly, following the resurrection Jesus instructs Peter three times to care for his flock (i.e., the community of disciples) as a demonstration of his love for Jesus (21:15–17). This threefold questioning and instructing of Peter after the resurrection clearly recalls Peter's threefold denial of Jesus (18:15–18, 25–27) just before the crucifixion. Indeed, Jesus had predicted the denial immediately after issuing the new commandment:

> "I give you a new commandment, that you love one another. Just as I have loved you, you also should love one another. By this everyone will know that you are my disciples, if you have love for one another."

> Simon Peter said to him, "Lord, where are you going?" Jesus answered, "Where I am going, you cannot follow me now; but you will follow afterward." Peter said to him, "Lord, why can I not follow you now? I will lay down my life for you." Jesus answered,

"Will you lay down your life for me? Very truly, I tell you, before the cock crows, you will have denied me three times." (13:34–38, NRSV)

- As this prediction scene connects Peter's denial with his inability to follow Jesus where he is going (i.e., crucifixion), so in the postresurrection scene Jesus predicts Peter's martyrdom and punctuates the prediction with the command "Follow me" (21:18–19). Indeed, Jesus' postresurrection prediction of Peter's martyrdom also echoes back to his warning in the farewell discourse that the disciples would face the same persecution he was about to face (15:18–21; 16:2–4, 33).

- As Jesus speaks of his departure, he promises that the Paraclete (Gk. *parakleton*) will come in his stead (14:16–18, 26; 15:26; 16:7–15). One sign of this promise is the peace that Jesus leaves with the disciples (14:27; see also 16:33). When the risen Jesus appears to the disciples the first time, he greets them, "Peace be with you" twice (for a third greeting, see also 20:26) and then gives them the Holy Spirit (20:19–22).

- The juxtaposition of grief and rejoicing occurs in several places in the farewell discourse (14:27–28; 15:11; 16:6–7; 17:13) but is most explicit in 16:16–24. Jesus tells the disciples that in a little while they will no longer see him, but then a little while later they will. Accompanying their inability to see Jesus (i.e., following the crucifixion) will be weeping, and following their renewed ability to see Jesus (i.e., after the resurrection) they will rejoice. At the empty tomb Mary Magdalene weeps because she believes that someone has taken the body of Jesus (20:11, 13, 15). This mourning is replaced by rejoicing when Jesus appears to the disciples (20:20).

- Just before Jesus moves from speaking to the disciples to praying on their behalf, he says, "The hour is coming, indeed it has come, when you will be scattered, each one to his home, and you will leave me alone" (16:32). While the primary reference for this scattering is the passion, where Jesus faces the cross alone, it is after the resurrection that Peter returns to Galilee and to his livelihood of fishing (21:1–3).

The farewell discourse leads the readers into the pathos of the passion narrative. But the verbal and thematic connections between the farewell discourse and the resurrection narrative that we have noted also allow the discourse to point beyond the passion to the resurrection. In other words, even before it occurs in the narrative, the passion is overshadowed by the resurrection–not canceled out but certainly upstaged somewhat. While the cross marks the beginning of the moment of Jesus' (and therefore God's) glorification, the resurrection and ascension (to which Jesus alludes during the farewell discourse) mark the conclusion of Jesus' return to God.

Passion Narrative

Turning from the farewell discourse to the passion narrative, we find that there are not as many verbal links between this section and the resurrection narrative. But neither are they necessary. No case needs to be made for the readers to recognize that the story of the resurrection flows out of the story of the arrest, trials, and crucifixion, especially after the passion, resurrection, and ascension have been interpreted as Jesus' departure during the farewell discourse.

In chapters 18–19 readers discover the culmination of the conflicts between Jesus and "the Jews," that is, the Jewish authorities. As with Matthew, most Johannine scholars argue that one of the primary issues that John is addressing is the conflict between Judaism and Christianity in his own day. This conflict gets anachronistic expression in the gospel in the form of believers in Jesus getting expelled from the synagogue (e.g., 9:22, 34; 12:41–43) and in the Jewish authorities' role in Jesus' execution. Throughout much of the first half of the gospel, the authorities have been plotting against Jesus (7:1, 25, 32, 44–52; 8:59; 10:31–39; 11:45–57). It is only when Judas, whom Satan enters, betrays Jesus that their plots meet with success (13:22–30; 18:1–11).

But following on the heels of the farewell discourse, in which Jesus embraces his departure as the glorification of himself and his Father as well as his return to the Father, the passion narrative does not read like a success story for the Jewish authorities at all. Indeed, readers get the sense that Jesus, and not the powers-that-be, is really in control. The narrator conveys this impression in numerous ways:

- When the chief priests, Pharisees, and police come to arrest Jesus, he walks out to meet them (18:4).

- When Jesus claims that there is no need to question him because he has taught publicly before the Jews, a guard strikes him for the manner in which he has spoken to the high priest. But Jesus simply claims that he has spoken rightly and gives no impression of being intimidated (18:19–24).

- In his exchanges with Pilate, Jesus demonstrates his power in a significant manner. First, when Pilate begins to question him, asking if he is the King of the Jews, Jesus responds by questioning Pilate in a challenging fashion: "Do you ask this on your own, or did others tell you about me?" (18:34). Second, when Pilate, exasperated by Jesus' refusal to answer him, claims to have the power to release or crucify Jesus, Jesus quickly puts Pilate in his place: "You would have no power over me unless it had been given from above [Gk. *anothen*]" (19:11).

- In the synoptics, when Jesus is taken to Golgotha, Simon of Cyrene is forced to carry Jesus' cross (Mt. 27:32; Mk. 15:21; Lk. 23:26). By contrast, John emphatically states that Jesus carried the cross "by himself" (Gk. *bastazon heato ton stauron*; 19:17).

- While hanging on the cross, Jesus conducts his final business: making sure that his mother is cared for (19:26–27).

- Jesus even, or especially, seems to be in control of his death. It is only when he sees that all is finished that he first claims to be thirsty, in order to fulfill scripture, and then declares aloud, "It is finished." In language that contradicts a view that Jesus' life was taken from him, the narrator announces Jesus' death scene by saying that

Jesus "gave up [or *handed over*] his spirit" (Gk. *paredoken to pneuma*). And by choosing the timing of his own death, Jesus ensures as well that his bones are not broken, thus fulfilling scripture again (19:28–37).

Thus, while the passion narrative is certainly full of pathos related to Jesus' suffering, Jesus is in no way presented as a helpless victim of the Jewish authorities. His martyrdom is chosen. He willingly lays down his life for his friends (see 15:13). Instead of losing to those plotting against him, the cross represents victory because it brings about the glorification of God and Jesus as well as initiating Jesus' return to God. This prepares the readers to understand the resurrection narratives not as an overturning of the results of the crucifixion, but as a continuation of them.

Resurrection in the Context of John's Theology

In the same manner that we have located the resurrection narrative in its narrative context, it is important that we locate it within its theological context within the gospel as well. One of the most significant differences between John's and the synoptic gospels' approach to the resurrection is actually found in the narrative material preceding the Easter story. While in the synoptics Jesus does predict his passion and resurrection, and thus foreshadows his fate beforehand, in John resurrection is a major theme throughout the narrative (2:1, 18–22; 3:13, 14; 5:21, 25–29; 6:62; 7:33; 8:14, 28; 12:23–26, 32; 13:1, 3, 33, 36; 14:2–7, 12, 28; 16:5–11, 16; 17:11). As such, the theme does much more than simply foreshadow the ending of the narrative. The emphasis on resurrection throughout the narrative interprets Jesus' resurrection before it even occurs within the plot. This is similar to Luke's interpretation of the resurrection in the speeches in Acts after the ascension, but in the case of John the interpretation is reordered: Jesus interprets the resurrection before it occurs. Let us briefly examine some of the theological emphases concerning resurrection.

In some early Christian traditions the resurrection is presented as the point at which Jesus becomes Lord as a result of his exaltation to the right hand of God. This is certainly not the case in John. The gospel of John begins with a prologue (1:1–18) that provides the reader insight into the origins (or better, lack of origins) and identity of Jesus: "In the beginning was the Word and the Word was with God and the Word was God." Clearly, the narrative that follows is to be about someone who is more than a prophet, indeed is more than a messiah. Jesus is the preexistent Word (Gk. *logos*) made incarnate. This is a much higher christology than Mark's, where Jesus is anointed as the Messiah at his baptism, or even than Matthew's and Luke's christology, where Jesus is conceived by the Holy Spirit. The Word is the agent of creation (existing before any *thing* existed) and as such is divine ("The Word was *with* God and the Word *was* God"). This Word becomes flesh; this Word becomes/is Jesus. While John's understanding of Christ does not represent a full-blown Trinitarian theology, it does clearly foreshadow such a development. One cannot overemphasize the importance of this incarnational theology for understanding John and its resurrection narrative. Instead of effecting the exaltation of Jesus to a divine status, the resurrection brings about Jesus' *return* to the preexistent state of being with God (e.g., 7:33; 13:3; 16:5). Therefore, the resurrection does *not* effect a change in Jesus' status. The significance of the resurrection must be found elsewhere.

Actually, the key to understanding the significance John attributes to Jesus' resurrection is found in the story in which Jesus raises Lazarus from the dead (11:1–54). This is the final sign that Jesus performs before his passion. As Jesus approaches Lazarus' home, Martha meets Jesus and argues that if Jesus had arrived earlier, her brother would not have died. She asks him to request that God do something even now, after the fact. Jesus' response is that Lazarus will rise again. As with others in John's gospel who interpret Jesus' words in a literal fashion (see below), Martha agrees that Lazarus will participate in the resurrection at the last day. But Jesus clarifies what he means with one of the many direct *I am* statements in the Fourth Gospel: "I am the resurrection and the life" (11:25). The healing that follows, then, is less about Jesus' power to bring someone back from the dead than it is a symbolic action narrated in support of Jesus' metaphorical claim about himself. In other words, this whole scene foreshadows not only Jesus' own resurrection, but ultimately reveals his own identity *as* resurrection and life. Thus, before the readers even reach the resurrection narrative, they are already told that the significance of Jesus' resurrection lies in its power to reveal that Jesus is the resurrection, *our* resurrection (see also 5:21–29). In other words, the Christ Event, reaching its culmination in the story of the resurrection, offers a life of eternal quality and significance to those who will participate in it.

While the Jewish authorities had been plotting against Jesus before this point in the narrative, it is following Lazarus' resurrection that their plan to put Jesus to death is expressed most emphatically (11:45–53). They fear that this self-revelatory sign will result in belief in Jesus that they cannot control, which in turn will result in the destruction of the nation. Through the Lazarus story, John turns the pattern of the story of the Christ Event on its head so that resurrection precedes crucifixion. Instead of primarily presenting God as responding to the crucifixion with resurrection, John portrays the Jewish authorities as responding to resurrection by killing Jesus. It is not the scandal of the cross but Jesus' life-giving nature symbolized in his resurrection that is the radical message of the Fourth Gospel.

Life

As mentioned earlier, the Johannine narrator describes the purpose of the gospel in the midst of the resurrection narratives:

> Now Jesus did many other signs in the presence of his disciples, which are not written in this book. But these are written so that you may come to believe that Jesus is the Messiah, the Son of God, and that through believing you may have life in his name. (Jn. 20:30–31, NRSV)

As the NRSV notes, in some ancient manuscripts we find "continue to believe" (Gk. *pisteuete*) instead of "come to believe" (Gk. *pisteusete*) in verse 31. We have already noted that John's gospel appears to have been written to undergird the faith of his community as they defined themselves over against the synagogue with whom they were in conflict. Therefore, regardless of which wording is original, the support and shaping of Christians' faith instead of conversion to Christianity is implied in this purpose statement.

Indeed, this declaration of intent makes clear to the reader that the narrator has not reported all that is known of Jesus' ministry. The author has been selective in choosing what to include in the Fourth Gospel (see also 21:25). The criterion by which scenes were chosen was the support of faith, specifically faith that leads to life. This connection between faith and life is strongly emphasized throughout the gospel (3:15, 36; 5:24; 6:40, 47; 11:25–26). The key question for the interpreter is how to understand what is meant by "life" in the narrative.

To answer this question, we must note the way that John uses irony. As we have already noted, the Fourth Gospel begins with the prologue (1:1–18), which allows the readers to enter the narrative with the knowledge that Jesus is the preexistent, divine, incarnate Word. The irony is established, of course, by the fact that the characters with whom Jesus interacts do not know the full depth of Jesus' identity as described for the readers. The narrator uses the characters' ignorance to invite the readers into an ever-deeper understanding of the Christ Event and its significance. Characters are repeatedly presented as misunderstanding Jesus' words because they do not fully know who he is. Their mistake is to take Jesus' words literally, when his speech is clearly meant to be understood as metaphorical–clearly, that is, for anyone who knows Jesus' real identity.

In addition to our earlier note about Martha's misunderstanding of Jesus' words about Lazarus' rising, two examples that appear early in the narrative will suffice to illustrate this literary technique. First, in chapter 3, Nicodemus, a pharisaic leader of the Jews, comes to Jesus under the cover of night. He admits that Jesus must be "from God" but nevertheless calls him simply Rabbi/teacher, thus showing the readers that he does not fully understand Jesus' significance. When Jesus tells him that one cannot see the dominion of God without being born again (Gk. *anothen*), Nicodemus misunderstands and interprets Jesus' words to mean literally being born *again,* that is, entering back into the mother's womb and starting over. Jesus, of course, means one must be born *from above,* that is, born of the Spirit. Later in chapter 4, when Jesus enters into dialogue with the Samaritan woman, she at first only knows him as a Jewish man. Jesus claims that if she knew his full identity she would ask for and receive "living water" that would keep those who drink it from ever being thirsty again. As with Nicodemus, the woman misunderstands Jesus' words by interpreting them in a literal fashion. Unlike Nicodemus, however, the woman is presented as coming to a fuller understanding of who Jesus is by the end of the scene (vv. 25–26, 29).

Analogous to Mark's use of parables, through these and other such cases of misunderstanding on the part of characters in the narrative (e.g., 2:18–22; 4:31–38; 6:30; 7:27, 35, 41–52; 8:31–33; 10:6, 33; 11:11–14) John's readers are encouraged to interpret not only Jesus' words but the whole of John's gospel in a metaphorical fashion and thus to grow in their own understanding of Jesus' identity.

Therefore, when we explore what John means by "life" in his assertion that the goal of his gospel is to create/support faith that leads to life, we should expect to discover a metaphorical and not a literal meaning. At the very beginning of the narrative, in the prologue, John's concern for the "life" of his readers is found in the statement that what came into being in the Word "was life, and the life was the light of the people" (1:4; see also 8:12). Thus, the readers hear from the beginning that this "life," which the Word creates, is revelatory (the contrast between light and darkness is also found in 3:19–21; 11:9–10; 12:35–36, 45–46). This revelatory character is further described as "eternal life" (3:15, 16, 36; 4:14, 36; 5:24; 6:27, 40, 47, 54, 68; 10:28; 12:25, 50; 17:2, 3). By "eternal life" John, however, means much more than literal immortality, or life after death. Indeed, the metaphor of eternal life is defined at the end of the farewell discourse where Jesus shifts from addressing the disciples to offering a prayer on their behalf. The prayer begins in this manner:

> Father, the hour has come; glorify your Son so that the Son may glorify you, since you have given him authority over all people, to give eternal life to all whom you have given him. And this is eternal life, that they may know you, the only true God, and Jesus Christ who you have sent. (17:1–3)

The fact that Jesus' own prayer refers to "Jesus Christ" shows that this is one of those many places where the narrator's voice merges with Jesus' voice in the Fourth Gospel and thus highlights its importance for explicating Johannine theology (compare 3:16ff.). It is clear from the opening of Jesus' prayer that John defines eternal life not in terms of the length of life (i.e., immortality) but in terms of the quality of existence. Eternal life *is* knowledge of God through Christ, not the *result* of knowing God through Christ (as many who speak of getting into heaven today would have us believe). The intent of John's gospel, therefore, is to point out for its readers the opportunity to experience this life that is Christ, to point to *our* (i.e., the readers') experience of Jesus Christ as resurrection, to point to our being born from above by the Spirit.

Like Luke–Acts, John strives to explain Jesus' post-crucifixion presence with the church by means of the Holy Spirit. While John has no ascension scene equivalent to Luke 24:50–51 or Acts 1:9–11, Jesus' ascension and return to the state of preexistent glory with the Father are strongly emphasized and are indeed a necessary part of an incarnational theology offered in a time when Jesus is no longer physically present (e.g., 3:13; 6:62; 12:32; 13:1; 14:3; 17:5, 11, 13; 20:17). Indeed, in John it is clear that Jesus' continuing presence with the church in the Spirit is not possible without the resurrection and ascension. As Jesus is sent by God, so is the Spirit sent by God and Jesus (1:33; 3:34; 7:39; 14:15–17, 25–28; 15:26; 16:7–15; 20:22) *when* Jesus returns to God. Again, the interpreter should not read into this assertion a full-blown Trinitarian theology, but a developmental prelude to it.

As we have noted, in the farewell discourse John uses the Greek word *parakletos* to describe the Holy Spirit (14:16–17, 26; 15:26; 16:7–15). The noun *Paraclete* has many possible meanings: one who comforts, exhorts, helps, encourages, intercedes. John seems to embrace this full range of nuances in his understanding of the role of the Holy Spirit as the continuing presence of Jesus in the community of faith. All these functions are necessary for Jesus to continue giving eternal life to those who believe. By reminding the church of what Jesus has taught

(14:26) and indeed who Jesus is (15:26) and by continuing the revelation that comes from God through Jesus (16:12–15), the Paraclete offers life to those in the community (6:63). Without the resurrection, this eternal life is not available to believers. With an eye to understanding the symbolic prelude to the community of readers receiving the Spirit-given eternal life, we now turn to John's resurrection narrative.

Resurrection Narrated

Although we have spoken of the two chapters that make up John's resurrection narrative, the postcrucifixion text is best divided into three sections based on the change in setting. The first scene focuses on the empty tomb (20:1–18); the second takes place in a house in Jerusalem (20:19–29); and the third occurs by the Sea of Tiberias in Galilee (21:1–23).

At the Tomb

John has detailed the care that was given at Jesus' burial, so when Mary Magdalene comes to the tomb, she comes to mourn and honor Jesus, not to complete his burial. When she finds the stone rolled away, she runs back to Simon and the disciple whom Jesus loved and declares that "they" (without specifying whom she thinks *they* are) have taken Jesus' body. As she ran to them, so then do Peter and the beloved disciple run back to the tomb. The beloved disciple outruns Peter, but Peter is the first to enter the tomb. He finds the linen cloths that had been used to wrap Jesus' head and body folded and lying in two separate places. The beloved disciple follows Peter into the tomb, sees, and believes. Then the disciples return home.

At this point Mary Magdalene returns to center stage. We are not told of her journey back to the tomb, only that she is standing outside it weeping. This time she looks in, and she sees two angels who were not there when Peter and the beloved disciple investigated. Unlike the figures at the tomb appearing to the women in the other gospels, these angels do not proclaim the resurrection. Instead, they only ask Mary why she is weeping. For a second time, she claims that "they" have taken Jesus' body, and she does not know where. At this point Jesus himself appears to Mary outside the tomb, but she does not recognize him and thinks him to be a gardener. When he echoes the angels and asks why she is weeping, Mary changes her assertion that they took Jesus into a request, "If you have carried him away, tell me where..." This shift shows that she assumes that this unknown gardener is part of the "they" to whom she has been referring, part of the conspiracy that took away Jesus. Recalling Jesus' words that the shepherd "calls his own sheep by name and leads them out" (10:3), the narrator presents Jesus as calling Mary by name, at which point she finally recognizes him. Upon Mary's recognition, Jesus instructs her not to "hold on" (Gk. *me mou haptou*) to him because his ascension to God is not complete. Mary then goes and tells the disciples, "I have seen the Lord."

While a short summary such as this highlights the movement of 20:1–18, it cannot do justice to the subtle theological and literary nuances of the section. Most important among these is the connection between *seeing* on the one hand and *knowing* and *believing* on the other, not dissimilar from the use of language of seeing in Mark's empty tomb scene. Note how many times sight is mentioned in John's version:

- Mary *saw* the rolled-away stone (v. 1) but did not *know* where they had taken her Lord (v. 2).
- The disciple whom Jesus loved bent down outside the tomb and *saw* the linen cloths lying inside (vv. 4–5).
- When Peter arrived, he entered the tomb and *saw* the cloths lying in separate places (vv. 6–7).
- At this point, the beloved disciple also entered and *saw* the cloths and *believed* (v. 8). The nature of this faith based on seeing the empty tomb is unclear, especially because John follows up the mentioning of his faith by saying, "for as yet they did not *understand* the scripture, that he must rise from the dead" (v. 9).
- As did the beloved disciple, Mary bent down outside the tomb and looked in. She *saw* two angels sitting at the head and foot of where Jesus' body had been (v. 12). But she still claimed that she did not *know* where they had taken and laid her Lord (v. 13).

- When Mary *saw* Jesus, she did not *know* it was him
  (v. 14).
- And, finally, when Mary proclaimed the good news of
  Jesus' resurrection to the disciples, she did not say, "The
  Lord is risen." She said, "I have *seen* the Lord" (v. 18).

When Mary focuses on the wrong things, she is unable to
see Jesus. But like the beloved disciple, when she finally sees,
she believes. This connection between sight and knowledge/
faith runs throughout John (e.g., 1:18, 50–51; 2:23; 3:3, 36; 6:2,
40, 62; 7:3; 9:1–41; 11:9, 40; 12:45; 14:7, 9, 17, 19; 16:10, 16–
19, 22; 17:24; 19:35). But we must not miss the way the
connection is used in service of John's theology of the
resurrection. The import of the resurrection has less to do with
changing Jesus' status than it does with *revealing* Jesus' status as
Lord. What is emphasized is not the raising of Jesus–we are
told nothing about *how* this occurs. What is emphasized is
Mary's *experience* of Jesus' resurrection.

Behind Closed Doors

This same emphasis is found in 20:19–29. The scene takes
place on the evening of the same day. Instead of being outside
the tomb, however, the disciples are hiding inside, behind
locked doors, in fear of the Jews. Jesus suddenly appears to
them in spite of the locked doors and greets them, "Peace be
with you." After he shows them his wounds, they rejoice that
they "*saw* the Lord." At this point Jesus repeats his greeting,
"Peace be with you." This time, however, the greeting is a
prelude to commissioning. He sends out the disciples as God
sent him. And as God breathed the Spirit into the human in
Genesis 2, so Jesus breathes on the disciples and gives them
the Holy Spirit, whom he has claimed gives life (6:63). Along
with the Spirit comes the authority to forgive and retain sins.

Thomas was not with the other disciples when all this
occurred, so they report to him what has happened using the
same language Mary had earlier used: "We have *seen* the Lord."
But Thomas claims that he himself must *see* the wounds and
touch them (Gk. *bal ton daktulon mou,* literally "place my finger"
into the wounds) or he will not *believe* (20:25). So a week later,
when Jesus appears again in the house, he greets the disciples

with "Peace be with you" and then shows Thomas his wounds, offers to let him touch them (Gk. *phere ton daktulon sou*), and says, "Do not doubt but *believe*." At this point Thomas goes further than anyone else in the narrative of the Fourth Gospel by calling Jesus "My Lord and my God!" (20:28). Jesus' response to this profession of faith is, "Have you *believed* because you have *seen* me? Blessed are those who have not *seen* and yet have come to *believe*."

Interpreters have long been too hard on Thomas for requiring sight as proof for belief. Indeed, in light of the fact that the beloved disciple, Mary, and the disciples behind closed doors all believe *because* they see, we must look for a more sympathetic interpretation of Jesus' reply to Thomas. In the context of chapter 20, this reply is clearly not a rebuke of Thomas, but is instead an affirmation of the readers. This blessing in turn enables the readers to affirm the purpose of the gospel that is described in the verses that follow: to support their faith, through which they (i.e., we) have life (vv. 30–31).

By the Sea

Although we have argued that chapter 21 should be read as an integral part of the narrative of John, the fact that it is separated from the Easter narrative in chapter 20 by the statement of purpose in 20:30–31 does give the reader a sense of a break between the Jerusalem epiphanies and the one in Galilee. Indeed, it is enough of a break that John does not even narrate the move of the disciples from Galilee to Jerusalem, but simply starts up with Peter, Thomas, Nathanael, James, John, and two others (one of whom is presumably the disciple whom Jesus loved; see v. 7) gathered at the Sea of Tiberias. Peter decides to go fishing, and the others join him.

Following their night of failure, the risen Jesus appears on the shore and tells them to cast their nets on the other side of the boat. It is not until they do so and catch more fish than they can pull into the boat that one of them, the beloved disciple, recognizes that it is Jesus. When he tells Peter that "it is the Lord!" Peter dresses himself, jumps into the water, and swims ashore. Jesus is there cooking for them and tells Peter to bring some fish. When Peter pulls the net ashore, it has 153 fish in it, but the net does not tear.

After they eat, Jesus asks Peter if he loves him more than the others. When Peter answers that he does love Jesus, Jesus tells him to feed his lambs. This question-and-answer sequence is repeated two more times, after which Jesus predicts that Peter will be martyred as an old man. Jesus punctuates the scene with the words "follow me." Peter, however, does not let the scene end on this note. When he sees the disciple whom Jesus loved, Peter asks about his fate, that is, if he would also be martyred. But Jesus refuses to allow Peter to move the focus from himself and again says, "Follow me."

The key to gaining entry into a legitimate interpretation of this scene is the recognition that Peter and the other disciples' going fishing does not represent a recreational activity, but the pursuit of a livelihood and therefore a failure to obey the sending forth by Jesus in 20:21. Thus, this final epiphany represents a correction. The risen Jesus appears, not to prove that the resurrection has occurred or to offer guidance, but to redirect the lives of the disciples in the postresurrection era.

The closest parallel to John's epiphany by the sea is Luke 5:1–11. In this story, Jesus climbs into Simon Peter's boat and asks him to push away from the shore so that he might teach the crowd standing on the shore. After he has finished speaking, he instructs Peter to sail out to deeper water and let down the nets. Peter informs Jesus that they had fished all night with no success, but that at his command he will try once more. This time, of course, there is great success. The nets become too full of fish for Peter to pull in without the help of another boat. Upon seeing this miracle, Peter falls on his knees in amazement and confesses his sinfulness to Jesus. But Jesus responds, "Do not be afraid; from now on you will be catching people." By placing John's story alongside Luke's, we are clued in to the fact that John 21:1–14 is not simply a postresurrection epiphany, but is part of a call narrative that extends through verse 23. The miraculous catch of fish simply focuses Peter's attention on Jesus, so that Jesus can then finally say, "Follow me."

The ending of John, therefore, points to a new beginning, the beginning of the church. This becomes obvious in the dialogue between Jesus and Peter in verses 15–19. Preachers have made much of the different Greek words for love used in this dialogue. The first two times Jesus asks Peter "do you love" using the verb *agapao,* which is often interpreted as unconditional love. Peter responds that he does love Jesus, but he uses the verb *phileo,* often taken to mean familial love, as it means in the name of the city *Philadelphia,* the city of brotherly love. Preachers take this to imply that Peter is unable to love Jesus unconditionally. The third time Jesus asks Peter whether he loves him, Jesus switches verbs and uses *phileo.* Following this, John writes, "Peter felt hurt because he said to him the third time, "Do you love [*phileo*] me?" And, of course, Peter responds one more time that he does love (*phileo*) Jesus. It is hard to deny that there is much potential homiletical fodder in this use of vocabulary. The problem is that John often uses synonyms without any significant shift in meaning. Indeed, if preachers are to make much of the difference between *agapao* and *phileo,* they also must interpret the difference between "Feed [*bosko*] my lambs [*arnion*]" (v. 15), "Tend [*pomaino*] my sheep [*probaton*]" (v. 16), and "Feed [*bosko*] my sheep [*probaton*]" (v. 17). We've all heard many sermons on the difference in the "love" language in this passage, but how many Easter sermons have focused on the subtle theological differences between feeding and tending or between sheep and lambs?

Peter's distress concerning Jesus' third question should be interpreted based not on the fact that Jesus changes the word he uses for love but on the fact that he asks a *third* time. This threefold questioning recalls Peter's threefold denial during the passion narrative. Peter's distress is evoked by being reminded of having denied Jesus three times. This dialogue brings Peter back into the fold as the one who is to care for the fold.

Indeed, the focus of the interpreter should be on Peter's responsibility for the flock. In the farewell discourse, Jesus commanded the disciples to love one another (i.e., one another *within* the flock) and says that this communal love will be the sign to others that they are in fact Jesus' disciples. Now Jesus develops that command one step further by identifying love for him in the postascension era (i.e., when Jesus is no longer physically present) with caring for the community. But Jesus does not stop with Peter's responsibility for the community. He goes on to tell what price Peter must pay in fulfilling that responsibility: Peter will die the death of a martyr (vv. 18–19). With such a declaration, preachers must resist the temptation to preach the resurrection as triumph over death. As did Jesus' declaration of himself as the resurrection and his symbolic raising of Lazarus result in his crucifixion, so will Peter's experience of the risen Jesus eventually result in his death.

John presents the preacher with two perspectives on the resurrection of Jesus Christ that serve as a balance to each other. In the two scenes in chapter 20, the risen Jesus is seen in unexpected places and in unexpected ways. By recognizing that God's presence is revealed in places we do not usually look for the Divine, the quality of life (i.e., daily life) is raised up to the level of Ultimacy. On the other hand, chapter 21 should keep preachers from equating the quality of life to which John points with a pie-in-the-sky view of human existence. Peter is redeemed, called back into the fold, and called to care for the fold. But the quality of existence to which he is called will lead to his death.

Thus, John offers a real-life approach to the quality of life in his account of the resurrection of Jesus. It is not an otherworldly, afterlife approach to life. It is not an idyllic, monastic approach to life. It is the in-the-thick-of-it life that John's Easter stories metaphorically represent as the ultimately meaningful life. Preachers will do well to offer their congregations a vision of the resurrection of Jesus Christ (or better, of Jesus Christ as the resurrection) that accords with their experiences of the-thick-of-it all around them.

What You See Is What You Get (Jn. 20)

"What you see is what you get!" We all know what that means. It means that there is nothing more to be expected. You will get no more than what is being offered to you right now. It means take what you see or leave what you see, because you will get nothing better.

But if we turn this saying on its head, it can literally mean something else. "What you see is what you get" could mean "Perception is reality." In other words, what you get out of anything, out of all things, is dependent upon what you focus on. There might be more to see; there might be something else to see. But if you don't see it, you won't get it. You'll only get what you are able to see. What you see *is* what you get.

Have you ever seen that simple outline sketch that looks like a duck head? There's just the neck rising up into a fairly round head, with a dot for the eye in the middle of it, and the long rounded bill sticking out in front of it. You know, it's the same drawing that, if you look at it differently, the bill becomes ears sticking out the back of the head and instead of a duck you see a rabbit. What we focus on makes all the difference. What you see is what you get.

Mary Magdalene comes to the tomb to honor her dead master. She saw him buried, and she is in deep mourning, unable to stop her weeping. But when she arrives, she sees the stone rolled away from the entrance to the tomb. In shock she races back to Peter and the disciple whom Jesus loved and tells them not that the stone has been moved, but that Jesus' body has been stolen and she doesn't know where it is. The two men race to the tomb, go inside, and see the linen cloths lying where Jesus' body once was. The beloved disciple leaves believing, but we don't know what they say to Mary or even if they encounter her. However, we do find her again at the tomb after the disciples are gone. This time she looks into the tomb. Instead of just seeing linen cloths folded neatly, she sees two angels, who ask her why she is weeping. But in spite of this heavenly epiphany, she still says that her master has been taken and she does not know where. Finally, Jesus himself appears to Mary and also asks why she is weeping. But Mary is so focused on the death she saw only a couple of days earlier that she fails to see the risen Jesus in her midst and thinks he is the gardener. She is so focused on the fact that a cemetery is a place of death that she is unable to see the life that is right in front of her eyes. What you see is what you get.

Have you ever seen that simple black and white drawing that looks like a wine glass? It's wide at the top, then narrows to a fancy stem with various indents and finally flattens back out at the base of the glass. You know, it's the same drawing that, if you look at the background instead of the foreground, the outlines of the glass become the outlines of two silhouettes of faces looking at each other. The top of the glass comes down into two foreheads, the indents in the stem become eyes, noses, and mouths, and the base becomes the chins. What we focus on makes all the difference. What you see is what you get.

Thomas has been out somewhere but returns to the house in Jerusalem where the disciples are hiding behind locked doors out of fear of the Jewish authorities who arrested and killed Jesus. What a surprise he encounters when these other disciples tell him that they have seen Jesus. What would you think in such a situation? Are they hallucinating as a result of cabin fever, out of guilt for having deserted and denied Jesus, out of fear of having to face the Jewish authorities who arrested and killed Jesus? One songwriter imagines Thomas thinking that the other disciples have hallucinated out of wishful thinking. In a song titled, "Who Moved the Stone?" Thomas sings, "How can he be alive? How can you know that it's really him? Don't let your love blind your eyes to reality."[1] And Thomas has seen reality. He has seen Jesus suffer and die. This perception of Jesus as dead is his reality. To accept the news of their vision of a risen Jesus is to deny his own vision of the crucified Jesus. He isn't so much doubting their word as he is being faithful to his own experience of Jesus. He is so focused on the means by which Jesus died—the wounds in his hands, feet, and side—that he fails to comprehend the means by which he is alive. So…unless I see the wounds that killed him, I won't believe that the one you saw is Jesus; I won't have faith that he is alive. What you see is what you get.

You know, it doesn't seem to me that Mary and Thomas *refuse* to see. We shouldn't point our fingers at them as if they made bad choices. They were so focused on the death that was all around them that they were unable to see the life in their midst. Until…until something refocused their eyes. Jesus calls Mary by name, and like the sheep who hears its master's voice and follows, suddenly she recognizes Jesus and affectionately calls him "Rabbouni." Jesus puts his hands in front of Thomas' face and invites him to stick his fingers in the wounds, and suddenly Thomas worships Jesus, calling him "my Lord and my God." Sometimes, somehow, something outside of us grabs us by the ears and turns our head so that we suddenly see what we have always missed. Our perception is altered, so our reality changes. In other words, sometimes, somehow, something illuminates life in the midst of the shadow of death.

Once when I was in the purgatory that is called "youth ministry," a junior-high-aged girl gave me a postcard with some block-like shapes printed on it. She waited while I tried to interpret them. I couldn't. For the life of me, I could not figure out what the meaning of these symbols was. She was, of course, very amused by my struggle and finally couldn't stand it anymore. Excited to be able to one-up her youth director, she spouted out, "Focus on the spaces between the blocks, not on the blocks themselves, stupid." Well, I'm sure you've seen this drawing before. When you focus on the spaces in between, you find the word *Jesus*. To focus on the wrong thing is to miss Jesus. What you see is what you get.

I don't fully understand why women allow their husbands or boyfriends to abuse them emotionally, physically, or sexually. It's easy to sit in front of the television, watching the news report of another death caused by domestic violence, and say, "I would just leave." Or "I would call the police." I don't know all the reasons why women in such situations don't leave or call the police. But I think I know at least a small piece of the answer. It has to do with what those women are able to see, what they perceive when they look in the mirror.

I know one woman who years ago looked in the mirror, and what she saw was someone who was put on earth for the sake of men. She saw someone who was not as strong as men. Not as bright as men. Not worth the same pay as men. Not having the same freedom as men. Not having as much authority as men. Not created first like men. Not the head of the household like men. Not made in the image of the heavenly Father like men. Not mentioned by name in "mankind" like men. She saw someone who in her own eyes was only as valuable as a man valued her. She saw that because the society that raised her taught her to see that in the mirror.

So when her boyfriend mocked her and insulted her, she took it in stride. And when the boyfriend became her husband and the verbal abuse became paired with financial and physical abuse, she didn't like it but she tolerated it. She tolerated the yelling, the slapping, the pushing. She tolerated her clothes being thrown out on the lawn. She tolerated having her finger broken. Finally, she asked her minister what she should do, and *he* quoted Paul to her—"Love endures all things"—and she tolerated her husband some more. And indeed, her family and friends encouraged her to take her vow "until death do us part" seriously and stay. Of course, for her that death could have come quickly.

Finally she realized that all her life she had been taught to see in a mirror dimly. But when enough mirrors are thrown at you and broken into hundreds of pieces, you are confronted with the fact that you have lived a lie. And indeed, the truth shall set you free.

This woman found life in the cemetery of her existence. She realized that the stone had been rolled away and that hope was right there beside her—she just hadn't recognized it. With little support from others, she left her house and almost all of her belongings and started over.

There were, of course, many years of painful transition. There were many reasons to be bitter toward the world. There were many opportunities to take from the world all that she could. But now that woman has committed much of her life to changing the perception that shapes the reality of other women who are in abusive situations. She helps them to break the mirrors that distort their self-image instead of waiting for those mirrors to be smashed over their heads. She points out hope. She shows them alternatives. She presents them with a vision of new life.

And every time she gets a call at two o'clock in the morning, and I watch her make arrangements for another woman to begin the liberation process she went through, I realize I am not simply watching my wife do her job. "Mary turned and said to him in Hebrew, 'Rabbouni!'" "Thomas answered him, 'My Lord and my God!'" What you see is what you get. Christ the Lord is risen today!

Happy Ever After (John 21:1–19)[2]

I don't trust stories that end with "And they lived happily ever after." Oh, I'd like to believe such endings, but they don't reflect reality, at least not the reality I know and live.

I guess that's why I have such a distaste for most of the Easter sermons I've ever heard. They turn the story of the empty tomb either into a syrupy-sweet message that equates resurrection with a panacea you can buy for $14.95 from the Home Shopping Network, or into a Francis Scott Key Christian national anthem filled with booming bass drums and blaring trumpets that announce the end of the red glare of Satan's rockets. Think about it: Did the last Easter sermon you heard transform the Creed to say, "and we believe in Jesus Christ, God's only son our Lord; who was conceived by the Holy Spirit, born of the virgin Mary; suffered under Pontius Pilate, was crucified, dead, and buried; on the third day he arose from the dead; and we live happily ever after"?

Easter sermons that proclaim Sunday morning hope without taking into account that Monday morning reality will reappear with the next sunrise transform the Easter story into a fairy tale. Fairy tales make for nice bedtime stories for small children, but are their endings trustworthy to describe the reality in which we experience and serve God? Didn't you ever wonder how many years Hansel and Gretel had to spend in counseling trying to cope with the posttraumatic stress from having almost become the witch's main course? And what happened when those three little pigs grew up to become three fat hogs living in that one small brick house?

Fairy tale endings just aren't trustworthy. I think that's why I like the Broadway musical *Into the Woods* so much. The first act begins, of course, with the words, "Once upon a time..." Suddenly the stage is filled with lots of different characters from lots of different fairy tales. Throughout the first act they all meet in the woods to resolve the conflicts of their individual tales. The last song of the first act is titled *Ever After,* and everything does seem happy: Cinderella has her prince, the baker and his wife have their child, and Jack has killed the giant. In fact, everything is so happy that the play feels like it's over. All through intermission while you're standing in line at the restroom, you're wondering, "What's left? What in the world can they do in the second act?"

But then the curtain rises to find that the prince is cheating on Cinderella; the once childless baker and his wife discover that their hut is too small for a family of three; and, worst of all, the wife of the giant that Jack killed comes down to earth to seek revenge for her husband's death. By the time the second act is over, marriages have ended, the town has been demolished, and several of the key characters have been killed. This act doesn't end with "happily ever after" like the first. But neither does it end in total despair. It's an ending that's a starting over: The surviving characters lay aside their self-centered concerns and band together to fight off the second giant. Afterward they band together to rebuild their lives. Finally, as the curtain closes, the widowed baker begins to tell his son the story of all that has happened. He ends the play with the same words with which the play began: "Once upon a time…" Now that's an ending I can trust. That mixture of hope and struggle describes the reality I know.

Regardless of the distorted message we have heard in so many Easter sermons, that's the kind of reality reflected in the New Testament stories of the resurrection. The ending of Mark never even tells of the disciples' seeing the risen Christ. A young man at the empty tomb tells the three women who have come to anoint Jesus' body that Jesus will meet the disciples back in Galilee. But because they are afraid, the women tell no one about either the empty tomb or the promise.

Matthew does go further than Mark by having Jesus appear to the disciples back in Galilee. However, no matter how much we might like him to do so, Jesus doesn't say to them, "Everything's going to be fine now. Go, live happily ever after." Instead, the one and only thing the resurrected Christ utters to the disciples is an order to get back to work: "Go, make disciples, baptize, teach."

The ending to Luke's resurrection story is the book of Acts. Jesus promises his disciples that the Holy Spirit will come upon them in Jerusalem to make them witnesses to the ends of the earth. And by the time the story is over, Stephen has been stoned, James has been beheaded, and Paul is awaiting trial before the emperor in Rome.

These three gospels do not end their stories of Jesus with "on the third day Jesus arose from the dead; and we live happily ever after." They each end with, "Once upon a time…" They end with a starting over. And the Fourth Gospel is no different in this respect. Chapter 21 of John is an epilogue that refuses to allow the story to end with an unrealistic happy-ever-after ending.

Peter and the disciples don't head down to the local watering hole to toast the victory of the resurrection. John doesn't tell us what the disciples are feeling and thinking, but doesn't the return to fishing seem to imply some sense of relief, relief that the whole Jesus thing has come to an end? Look at Peter: He's taken a few years out of his life and followed this fellow Jesus—listened to him speak wonderful words and watched him display amazing signs of his glory. But Peter also traveled from town to town without rest. He was caught in the middle of disputes between Jesus and the religious authorities. He misunderstood what Jesus was all about up to the point of denying him three times. And he saw his teacher executed. While in his old age he might become nostalgic for the days when he had followed Jesus, for now he can get back to living a normal life. Now he is able to return to the one thing he knows well: fishing—the good ol' simple, predictable business of fishing.

In a sermon at Yale Divinity School, William Muehl told of reading what a German soldier wrote in his journal after having just watched the defeated French army march back into Paris following France's surrender in World War II. To paraphrase, the soldier said, "I know that I am the victor and that I should be happy for my country, but I envy these French soldiers. They may have lost the war, but at least they don't have to fight anymore. As they return to their plows and typewriters, I will still be carrying this gun." When the fight seemed over, Peter returned to his simple, normal livelihood as quickly as possible.

But then the resurrected Jesus calls a miraculous breakfast meeting and makes his announcement to Peter and the others: "It's not over...it's anything but over...it's just getting started...and you've got to get back out there and get back to it." "Do you love me? Feed my sheep." Then Jesus says to Peter, "Follow me," as if he were calling him to be a disciple for the very first time. This doesn't sound like an ending. This sounds like the beginning.

If Jesus hadn't already ruined Peter's day when he told him that his responsibility for Jesus' flock was just beginning, he certainly did when he told him what the result of his starting over would be: "Your pastoral care, your evangelization, your traveling from town to town, your disputes with the authorities will get you the great big reward of martyrdom." Now do you think the great apostle, whose nickname is Rock, takes this news well and interprets it as a happy-ever-after ending? No way. He sees the beloved disciple walking by and asks Jesus, "What about him? Is he going to have to die too?" You know the saying, "Misery loves company." Well, at this moment, Peter knows misery. Not only does he not get to spend his days making a decent living by fishing, his days are going to be cut short.

John's gospel doesn't have a happy-ever-after ending. In fact, it doesn't really have an ending at all. It's a story about the real-life process of starting over that is part of the wonder of the human condition. It's a story that reflects the reality that we as Christians, that we as human beings, know and live. It's a story that foreshadows the mixture of success and failure, of hope and struggle we should all expect. It's a resurrection story. It's our story.

Preachers who tell the Easter story as if it begins with nothing in the tomb but an echo and ends with a wake that is transformed into a reunion tell only a half-truth. Our story of the resurrection doesn't help us to escape from the world. It leads us back into the world, struggling with hope to start over with the work of Christ. Our story of the resurrection can be found repeating itself in our midst all the time.

Once upon a time, there were numerous volunteers who were working at a soup kitchen on Easter Sunday. They were working to prepare a special meal. Instead of the usual soup and sandwiches, the patrons of the shelter would eat baked ham, mashed potatoes, fresh green beans, yeast rolls, and chocolate cake. Among the volunteers who fed the unusually large crowd that Easter were two women who had recently become regular Sunday night volunteers. When the day was over and five thousand people had been fed and there were still twelve refrigerators full of leftovers, the two tired women walked out to their cars together. One of them said, "Can you believe so many people donated so much food? Can you believe we fed five thousand people? I feel a little better about the world and about myself right now. I think I'll be riding high on this for a long while." The other woman smiled and simply replied, "I'll see you, same time next week." And they lived...well, they *lived*.

Introduction

[1]This Turkish folktale is taken and paraphrased from Jane Yolen, ed., *Favorite Folktales from around the World* (New York: Pantheon, 1986).

Chapter 2

[1]While there are two other extant endings to the gospel of Mark (usually referred to as the shorter and longer endings), scholars agree that they are both later scribal attempts to resolve the seeming incompleteness of 16:1–8. Although they are in the minority, there are still a number of scholars who argue that 16:1–8 was not Mark's original ending, but the original is lost forever. This essay will work with the assumption that 16:1–8 was indeed Mark's close to his narrative.

[2]We refer to the author of the second gospel as "Mark" out of convention. The designation of the author as Mark was not original, and we do not know who the author actually was. We follow this pattern of convention with the other three gospels as well.

[3]C. H. Dodd, *The Parables of the Kingdom* (New York: Charles Scribner's Sons, 1935), 16.

[4]Some important ancient manuscripts do not include "the Son of God" (Gk. *huiou theou*) in 1:1, but the narrative evidence indicates that the phrase should be considered part of the original text.

[5]This sermon was originally published in O. Wesley Allen, Jr., *Good News from Tinyville: Stories of Hope and Heart* (St. Louis: Chalice Press, 1999), 28–35.

Chapter 5

[1]Sonny Salsbury, "Who Moved the Stone?" *Breakfast in Galilee* (Waco, Tex.: Word Music, 1978).

[2]A version of this sermon was originally published in *Lectionary Homiletics* 6 (1995): 43–44. It is used here with permission.

Allen, O. Wesley, Jr. *Good News from Tinyville: Stories of Hope and Heart*. St. Louis: Chalice Press, 1999.

Avis, Paul, ed. *The Resurrection of Jesus Christ*. London: Darton, Longman & Todd, 1993.

Barrett, C. K. *The Gospel According to St. John*. 2d ed. Philadelphia: Westminster Press, 1978.

Barton, Stephen C., and Graham N. Stanton, eds. *Resurrection: Essays in Honour of Leslie Holden*. London: SPCK, 1994.

Best, Ernest. *Mark: The Gospel as Story*. Edinburgh: T. & T. Clark, 1983.

Bode, E. L. *The First Easter Morning: The Gospel Accounts of the Women's Visit to the Tomb of Jesus*. Rome: Pontifical Biblical Institute, 1970.

Borg, Marcus J., and N. T. Wright. *The Meaning of Jesus: Two Visions*. San Francisco: HarperCollins, 1999.

Boring, M. Eugene. *The Gospel of Matthew: Introduction, Commentary, and Reflections*. Vol. 8, *The New Interpreter's Bible*. Nashville: Abingdon Press, 1995.

Brown, Raymond E. *The Gospel According to John*. Vol. 29/29A, The Anchor Bible. New York: Doubleday, 1966/1970.

——. *A Risen Christ in Eastertime: Essays on the Gospel Narratives of the Resurrection*. Collegeville, Minn.: Liturgical Press, 1991.

Bultmann, Rudolf. *The Gospel of John*. Philadelphia: Westminster Press, 1971.

——. *The Theology of the New Testament*. New York: Charles Scribner's Sons, 1955.

Carnley, Peter. *The Structure of Resurrection Belief*. New York: Clarendon Press, 1987.

Collins, Adela Yarbro. *The Beginning of the Gospel: Probings of Mark in Context*. Minneapolis: Fortress Press, 1992.

Craddock, Fred B. *Luke*. Interpretation. Louisville: Westminster/ John Knox Press, 1990.

Culpepper, R. Alan. *Anatomy of the Fourth Gospel: A Study in Literary Design*. Cambridge: Cambridge University Press, 1983.

———. *The Gospel of Luke: Introduction, Commentary, and Reflections.* Vol. 9, *The New Interpreter's Bible.* Nashville: Abingdon Press, 1995.

Danker, Frederick W. *Jesus and the New Age: A Commentary on St. Luke's Gospel.* Revised edition. Philadelphia: Fortress Press, 1988.

Davies, W. D., Jr., and Dale C. Allison. *A Critical and Exegetical Commentary on the Gospel According to Saint Matthew.* 2 vols. International Critical Commentary Series. Edinburgh: T. & T. Clark, 1988/1991.

Dodd, C. H. *The Parables of the Kingdom.* 3d ed. New York: Charles Scribner's Sons, 1936.

Evans, C. F. *Resurrection and the New Testament.* London: SCM Press, 1970.

Fitzmyer, Joseph A. *To Advance the Gospel.* New York: Crossroad, 1981.

———. *The Gospel According to St. Luke.* Vol. 28/28A, The Anchor Bible. New York: Doubleday, 1981/1985.

Fowler, Robert M. *Let the Reader Understand: Reader-Response Criticism and the Gospel of Mark.* Minneapolis: Fortress Press, 1991.

Frei, Hans W. *The Identity of Jesus Christ: The Hermeneutical Basis of Dogmatic Theology.* Philadelphia: Fortress Press, 1967.

———. *Theology and Narrative: Selected Essays.* Edited by George Hunsinger and William C. Placher. New York: Oxford University Press, 1993.

Fuller, Reginald H., and Pheme Perkins. *Who Is The Christ? Gospel Christology and Contemporary Faith.* Philadelphia: Fortress Press, 1983.

Gaffin, Richard B. *The Centrality of the Resurrection: A Study in Paul's Soteriology.* London/Grand Rapids, Mich.: Marshall, Morgan & Scott/Eerdmans, 1978.

Gundry, Robert H. *Mark: A Commentary on His Apology for the Cross.* Grand Rapids, Mich.: Eerdmans, 1993.

Gunter, W. Stephen. *Resurrection Knowledge: Recovering the Gospel for a Postmodern Church.* Nashville: Abingdon Press, 1999.

Harris, Murray J. *From Grave to Glory: Resurrection in the New Testament.* Grand Rapids, Mich.: Baker, 1990.

Harrison, Everett F. "The Resurrection of Jesus Christ in the Book of Acts and in Early Christian Literature." In

Understanding the Sacred text: Essays in Honor of Morton S. Enslin on the Hebrew Bible and Christian Beginnings. Edited by J. Reumann, 217–31. Valley Forge, Penn.: Judson Press, 1972.

Heil, John P. *Blood and Water: The Death and Resurrection of Jesus in John 18–21.* Washington, D.C.: Catholic Biblical Association, 1995.

———. *The Death and Resurrection of Jesus: A Narrative-Critical Reading of Matthew 26–28.* Minneapolis: Fortress Press, 1991.

Johnson, Luke Timothy. *The Acts of the Apostles.* Vol. 5, *Sacra Pagina.* Collegeville, Minn.: Liturgical Press, 1992.

———. *The Gospel of Luke.* Vol. 3, *Sacra Pagina.* Collegeville, Minn.: Liturgical Press, 1991.

———. *Living Jesus: Learning the Heart of the Gospel.* San Francisco: HarperCollins, 1999.

Kelber, Werner, ed. *The Passion in Mark.* Philadelphia: Fortress Press, 1976.

Kelsey, Morton. *Resurrection: Release from Oppression.* New York: Paulist Press, 1985.

Kingsbury, Jack Dean. *The Christology of Mark's Gospel.* Philadelphia: Fortress Press, 1983.

———. *Matthew as Story.* 2d ed. Philadelphia: Fortress Press, 1988.

Kysar, Robert. *John.* Augsburg Commentary on the Bible. Minneapolis: Augsburg, 1986.

Longenecker, Richard N., ed. *Life in the Face of Death: The Resurrection of the New Testament.* Grand Rapids, Mich./ Cambridge: Eerdmans, 1998.

Lorenzen, Thorwald. *Resurrection and Discipleship: Interpretive Models, Biblical Reflections, Theological Consequences.* Maryknoll, N.Y.: Orbis Books, 1995.

Luedemann, Gerd. *The Resurrection of Jesus.* Translated by John Bowden. Minneapolis: Fortress Press, 1994.

MacDonald, J. I. H. *The Resurrection: Narrative and Belief.* London: SPCK, 1989.

Marshall, I. Howard. "The Resurrection in the Acts of the Apostles." In *Apostolic History and the Gospel: Biblical and Historical Essays Presented to F. F. Bruce on His 60th Birthday.* Edited by W. W. Gasque and R. P. Martin, 92–107. Grand Rapids, Mich.: Eerdmans, 1970.

——. "The Resurrection of Jesus in Luke." *Tyndale Bulletin* 24 (1973): 55–98.

Martyn, J. Louis. *History and Theology of the Fourth Gospel.* 2d ed. Nashville: Abingdon Press, 1979.

Marxsen, W. *The Resurrection of Jesus of Nazareth.* Philadelphia: Fortress Press, 1970.

Moltmann, Jürgen. *The Future of Creation.* Philadelphia: Fortress Press, 1979.

——. *Jesus Christ for Today's World.* Translated by Margaret Kohl. Minneapolis: Fortress Press, 1994.

——. *Religion, Revolution and the Future.* Translated by M. Douglas Meeks. New York: Charles Scribner's Sons, 1969.

Montefiore, Hugh. *The Womb and the Tomb.* London: Fount, 1992.

Moule, C. F. D., ed. *The Significance of the Message of Resurrection for Faith in Jesus Christ.* London: SCM Press, 1968.

Myers, Ched. *Binding the Strong Man: A Political Reading of Mark's Story of Jesus.* Maryknoll, N.Y.: Orbis Books, 1988.

Neyrey, Jerome H. *The Resurrection Stories.* Wilmington, Del.: Michael Glazier, 1988.

Nolland, John. *Luke.* Word Bible Commentary. Dallas: Word, 1989–93.

O'Collins, Gerald. *Experiencing Jesus.* London: SPCK, 1994.

——. *Interpreting the Resurrection: Examining the Major Problems in the Stories of Jesus' Resurrection.* New York: Paulist Press, 1988.

——. *The Resurrection of Jesus Christ: Some Contemporary Issues.* Milwaukee: Marquette University Press, 1993.

——. *What Are They Saying About the Resurrection?* New York: Paulist Press, 1978.

O'Day, Gail R. *The Gospel of John: Introduction, Commentary, and Reflections.* Vol. 9, *The New Interpreter's Bible.* Nashville: Abingdon Press, 1995.

Osborne, Grant R. *The Resurrection Narratives: A Redactional Study.* Grand Rapids, Mich.: Baker, 1984.

Osborne, Kenan B. *The Resurrection of Jesus: New Considerations for Its Theological Interpretation.* New York: Paulist Press, 1997.

Perkins, Pheme. *The Gospel of Mark: Introduction, Commentary, and Reflection.* Vol. 8, *New Interpreter's Bible.* Nashville: Abingdon Press, 1995.

——. *Resurrection: New Testament Witness and Contemporary Reflection.* New York: Doubleday, 1984.

Perrin, Norman. *The Resurrection According to Matthew, Mark, and Luke.* Philadelphia: Fortress Press, 1977.

Rahner, Karl. *Theological Investigations.* Vol. 17. New York: Crossroad, 1981.

Russell, Letty M. *Becoming Human.* Library of Living Faith. Philadelphia: Westminster Press, 1982.

Schnackenburg, Rudolf. *The Gospel According to St. John.* 3 vols. New York: Seabury, 1982.

Senior, Donald. *The Passion of Jesus in the Gospel of Luke.* Collegeville, Minn.: Liturgical Press, 1992.

Smith, D. Moody. *The Theology of the Gospel of John.* Cambridge: Cambridge University Press, 1995.

Smith, Robert H. *Easter Gospels: The Resurrection of Jesus According to the Four Evangelists.* Minneapolis: Augsburg, 1983.

Sölle, Dorothee. *Beyond Mere Dialogue: On Being Christian and Socialist: Sin and Alienation, Cross and Class Struggle, Resurrection and Liberation.* Detroit: CFS, 1982.

Spong, John Shelby. *The Easter Moment.* San Francisco: Harper & Row, 1980.

——. *Resurrection Myth or Reality?: A Bishop's Search for the Origins of Christianity.* San Francisco: HarperCollins, 1994.

Talbert, Charles H. *Reading Luke: A Literary and Theological Commentary on the Third Gospel.* New York: Crossroad, 1982.

——. "The Place of Resurrection in the Theology of Luke." *Interpretation* 46 (1992): 19–30.

Tannehill, Robert C. *The Narrative Unity of Luke–Acts: A Literary Interpretation.* 2 vols. Philadelphia: Fortress Press, 1986.

Tillich, Paul. *Systematic Theology.* Vol 3. Chicago: University of Chicago Press, 1963.

Tolbert, Mary Ann. *Sowing the Gospel: Mark's World in Literary-Historical Perspective.* Minneapolis: Fortress Press, 1989.

Ulrich, Luz. *Matthew 1–7: A Commentary.* Minneapolis: Augsburg, 1989.

Wangerin, Walter. *Reliving the Passion: Meditations on the Suffering, Death and Resurrection of Jesus as Recorded in Mark.* Grand Rapids, Mich.: Zondervan, 1992.